Learn SQL Quickly

A Beginner's Guide to Learning SQL, Even If You're New to Databases

CodeQuickly.org

Table of Contents

This page intentionally left blank.

Chapter 1: Introduction

The information era is upon us, and the ability to organize and make sense of data has become an invaluable skill. Have you been hearing about data, databases, or SQL, and wondering what they are all about? Or perhaps you have just gotten a new job and need to learn SQL fast. If so, this book is for you. You no longer have to feel lost and overwhelmed by all of the fragmented tutorials online, nor do you have to waste your time and money learning SQL from lengthy books and expensive online courses.

1.1 - What this book offers

Concepts in this book are presented in a 'to-the-point' and concise style to cater to busy individuals. With this book, you can learn SQL in just one day and start coding immediately. Complex topics are broken down into simple steps with <u>clear and carefully chosen examples</u> to ensure that you can easily master SQL **even if you have never coded before**. In addition, the output for all examples are provided immediately, so you do not have to wait until you have access to your computer to test the examples. The complete process from database creation, table creation, data input, manipulation, and retrieval is covered. The flow of the book is carefully planned to ensure that you can easily follow along.

1.2 - How this book is different

The best way to learn SQL is by doing. This book provides examples for all concepts taught so that you can try the different SQL commands yourself. In addition, you will be guided through a complete project at the end of the book that requires the application of all of the concepts discussed. Working through the project will not only give you an immense sense of achievement, but it will also help you retain the knowledge and master the language.

1.3 - What you will learn:
- What is a database and DBMS?
- What is SQL?
- What software do you need to code SQL programs?

- How to create databases and tables in SQL.
- How to input data into the database.
- How to select data from SQL tables.
- How to use aggregate functions.
- How to write JOIN and UNION statements.
- What is a SQL view?
- How to write SQL triggers.
- How to write stored procedures and functions.
- How to make decisions with IF and CASE statements.
- How to control the flow of a program with WHILE, REPEAT, and LOOP statements.
- What are cursors?
- How to use cursors.

At the end of the book, you will be guided through a hands-on project that involves applying of all the topics discussed.

1.4 - What is a database?

The first question we must answer is a simple one: <u>What is a database?</u>
Briefly put, a database is a collection of related information. This is the most general definition of the word database. Some real-world examples include a phone book, a shopping list, a to-do list, your three best friends, or perhaps, the way in which most people think of databases, Twitter's entire collection of users. All of these illustrate what a database can be. All of these are collections of information that store related 'stuff.'

Databases can be stored in different ways. You can store a database on paper. If I had a shopping list or a to-do list, I might just scribble it down on a piece of paper. You can also store a database in your mind. Let's take the example from the previous paragraph of your three best friends. If you were asked to list your three best friends, it would be doubtful that you have this information written down. One simply can recall this data instinctively. You can store this information in your mind, just as you can store information on a computer. In most cases, when people are talking about creating a database, they are referring to the creation and hosting of a database on a computer.

Let's discuss how we can create databases on computers. Computers are excellent at storing information, making them an excellent candidate for hosting our databases. A database can be as simple as a text file that you have created using the notepad application on your computer. It can also be a Microsoft Excel file. However, in most cases, if you are going to be using a database, you will probably need to use a special type of software application which is designed to help you create and maintain a database. This software is called a **Database Management System (DBMS)**.

A DBMS is a special software program that helps users create and maintain a database on a computer, making it simple for users to manage large amounts of information.

DBMSs can also handle security, which means that only users that have the correct security credentials (their username and password) can access the data. A DBMS can also backup your data, as well as import and export data from other sources.

A DBMS is designed to create, store, and keep track of the information in our database. A clear distinction must be made here, as people often get confused about this, **the DBMS is not the actual database**. The DBMS is the software application that is creating, maintaining, updating, and deleting information from the actual database.

Let's consider eBay and how they might use a DBMS to manage their business, website, and products.

If you are a company like eBay with trillions of pieces of information that you need to keep track of, a DBMS is the perfect method of doing so.

eBay will interact with the DBMS to create, read, update, and delete information. eBay gives instructions to the DBMS and tells it what to do next. For example, imagine you are logging into your account on the eBay website. You simply enter your username and password and click the login button. This only works because programmers at eBay have written code that tells the computer to search for your username and password in the DBMS. After you click the login button, the

4

computer will search for your credentials, and, if found, will log you in. Think about other ways a company like eBay may use a DBMS!

Now that we have discussed DBMSs, we move on to learn about the two main types of databases that you will find in computing. The first is called a **relational database**. You will also hear people refer to these as SQL databases. The other type of database is called a **non-relational database**. We will look at the meaning of 'SQL' shortly, but first, we must determine the key differences between these two types of databases.

A relational database organizes data into one or more **tables**. Each table has columns and rows, and a **unique key** that identifies each row. Relational databases are by far the most popular type of database. When using relational databases, we store information in a structure called a **table.** A relational database is a lot like an Excel spreadsheet, where there are columns and rows that store information.

Now let's look at non-relational databases. A non-relational database is basically any type of database that **is not** a relational database. As mentioned previously, relational databases are far more popular and any other type of database that is not technically relational is just referred to as non-relational.

We can use a relational DBMS to help us create and maintain a relational database. Some of the most popular DBMSs are MySQL, Oracle, Postgres SQL, and Maria database. Relational DBMSs use something called **Structured Query Language (SQL)**. SQL is a standardized language for interacting with relational DBMSs. A relational DBMS is just a software application that we can use to create, maintain, and perform a variety of actions to our relational database. SQL is the language that we use to interact with those relational DBMSs. We can use SQL to perform **CRUD operations** as well as other administrative tasks like user management, security, and backup. Within computer programming, the acronym CRUD stands for create, read, update, and delete. These are the four basic functions of persistent storage.

We can use SQL to define tables and structures. A relational database uses tables to organize information. We use SQL to define those tables and then insert information into those tables. SQL is a standardized language; this means it is used practically on every relational DBMS. However, different relational DBMSs implement SQL with slight differences. Not all SQL code that you use on one relational DBMS will port over to another one without slight modifications.

1.5 What is SQL?

SQL is a language that is used for interacting with relational DBMSs. You might want to create a database for an application that you are building. The relational DBMS can ensure that the database is structured and stored correctly, but how do we retrieve this information and display it to a user that is using our application?

If we want to ask a relational DBMS to do something for us, SQL is the language that we can use to communicate with the DBMS. By using SQL to instruct our DMBS, we can create, retrieve, update, delete data, as well as create and manage different databases, design, and create database tables.

SQL has a specification and structure which defines how SQL needs to be used for the different commands to work as expected. However, the problem is that there are a variety of DBMSs out there. Some of the popular ones include Postgres, MySQL, Oracle, and Microsoft SQL Server. All these relational DBMSs implement SQL in slightly different ways. You can write SQL code that can work on one relational DBMS. However, if you tried to use it on another system, it might not work as you would expect. You might need to tweak a couple of things to get your SQL commands to work again.

SQL is a hybrid language. It is basically four types of languages nested into one. You will hear people mention these different terms, so it is valuable to know the meaning of each.

1. **SQL is a data query language**. This means it can be used to query the database for information. You can write queries (a collection of SQL commands) in SQL, which tell the relational DBMS what pieces of information you want to extract from the database. In conclusion, data query language is used to get data that is already stored in the database.

2. **SQL is a data definition language**. This means you can use SQL to define database schemas. A database schema is the overall layout and structure of the database. For example, what tables are going to be make up the database, what columns those tables are going to have, and the data types that those columns are going to be able to store.

3. **SQL is a data controlling language.** This simply means that it is used for controlling access to the data in the database. You can use it to configure permissions for different users. Correctly setting permissions for different users will ensure the integrity of your data.

4. **SQL is a data manipulation language.** It can be used for inserting, updating, and deleting data from the database. This will modify the stored data without affecting the database schema or database objects.

These are the four types of actions that you can perform with SQL. It is beneficial to understand these different actions that SQL can do, and how they are broken up into these four sections.

To show you SQL in action, we are going to install a relational DBMS called MySQL, which is one of the most popular DBMSs for beginners and experts alike.

But first, let's have a quick look at how MySQL compares to the alternative relational DBMSs that are available.

1.6 - MySQL vs. Alternatives

Oracle
The Oracle Corporation was the first company to develop a commercial version of SQL that was designed to manipulate data in a relational DBMS using queries. One of the primary reasons that the Oracle relational DBMS has maintained its popularity is the fact that its product updates are closely tied to changes in the market.

SQL Server

Microsoft SQL Server entered in the mid-1990s when Microsoft purchased it from Sybase. Similar to the Oracle Corporation, Microsoft has attempted to enhance SQL Server to keep up with changing technology. One of the new major features of SQL Server 2005 was support for XML (eXtensible Markup Language), which was a popular format at the time. This feature provided SQL Server with an advantage over their competitors, which further increased Microsoft SQL Server's popularity.

PostgreSQL

PostgreSQL has emerged as an open source relational DBMS and has gained popularity with some programmers. PostgreSQL is more specialized than MySQL. SQL has a standard that is uniform across several database engines. While PostgreSQL does follow many of the changes, it has a lot of additional coding that is not regulated as part of SQL standardization. When you are learning a language, it is best to learn a language that follows basic standards. PostgreSQL is an advanced type of SQL.

Ultimately, PostgreSQL only gives you an advantage when you are working with proprietary software (such as Oracle) because it more easily integrates their modifications. As a more advanced language, PostgreSQL is incredibly powerful, but not necessary in most instances. For most relational databases, simplicity is best because it is easier to review and make changes without requiring brushing up on the language and changes.

MySQL

MySQL was not originally developed for commercial use and it is an open source database. The Digital Age spawned a movement in software development collaboration that has blossomed into a competitive market for databases and other software. According to market reports, there is an excess of 10 million installations of MySQL, which indicates it is quickly moving into the enterprise space.

In Summary

Oracle and SQL Server are considered tools that favor users with large enterprise systems, while MySQL is considered a tool that appeals more to individuals interested in managing databases associated with their websites. As with Oracle and SQL Server, MySQL has released updates to its software just about every year. The main difference between the two open source systems, MySQL and PostgreSQL, is that PostgreSQL is a more advanced specialized tool, where many of its advanced features are not necessary for the most common database uses.

Feature	Oracle	SQL Server	Postgres	MySQL
Interface	GUI, SQL	GUI, SQL, Various	GUI, SQL	SQL
Language Support	Many, including C, C#, C++, Java, Ruby, and Objective C	Java, Ruby, Python, C#, VB,.Net, and PHP	Many including Perl, Python, Java, JavaScript, R, Ruby	Many including C, C#, C++, D, Java, Ruby, and Objective C
Operating System	Windows, Linux, Solaris, HP-UX,OSX, z/OS, AIX	Windows	Proprietary	Windows, Linux, OSX, FreeBSD, Solaris
Licensing	Proprietary	Proprietary	Open source	Open source

We will begin by writing SQL queries. These queries are used to query a database and interact with the database in a variety of ways.

Let's get started!

What would you like to accomplish by learning MySQL? Think about the big picture. What is your main goal? Is there a special project you'd like to achieve?

Chapter 2: Getting Started

2.1 - Learning Context

You are going to learn SQL using practical examples. By writing your own queries, you will experience the following benefits:

1. Real world applications – Experiential learning takes data and concepts and makes them 'real' by applying them to hands-on tasks, with real results. As you interact with the information, it becomes real. Your learning experience will be guided by your unique past experiences, which will make you interact with the information and the task in different ways.

2. Mistakes – Experiential learning involves trial by error. As you engage with these hands-on tasks, you will find that some approaches work better than others. You are sure to make mistakes throughout the course of this book; these mistakes are invaluable. Making mistakes is the only way one can learn.

3. Opportunity for creativity – Problems often have more than one solution. Experiential learning allows the student to engage with the material and seek their own unique and creative solution to the task at hand.

Useful Tip: Hands on learning – There is no better way to learn than by doing. Follow every example on your own and experiment your own examples.

2.2 - Installation

We are going to learn how to install MySQL server and MySQL Workbench onto your machine and how to connect the two together so that you can access your local server through MySQL Workbench. MySQL Workbench is a visual database design tool that integrates SQL development, administration, database design, creation, and maintenance into a single, integrated, development environment for the MySQL database system.

MySQL installer provides you with an easy-to-use wizard that helps you to install MySQL.

Follow the steps below to complete the installation:

1. To download MySQL installer, go to the following link: http://dev.mysql.com/downloads/installer/

2. Notice the Select Operating System drop-down menu. Select your operating system. Also note:

- If you have an online connection while running the MySQL Installer, choose the mysql-installer-web-community file.
- If you do NOT have an online connection while running the MySQL Installer, choose the mysql-installer-community file.

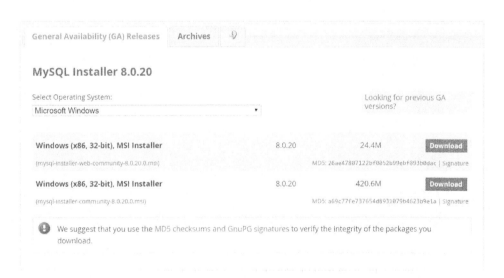

3. After clicking the 'download' button, the installer file should be downloaded. Click on this file:

mysql-installer-we....msi   ∧

4. You will be asked to Sign Up for an Oracle Web account. You can ignore this for now. On the bottom of the page, click the link 'No thanks, just start my download.'

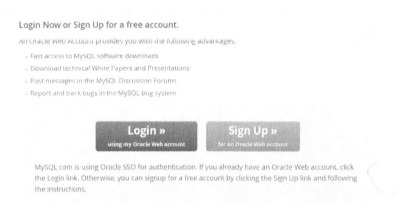

5. Select 'Developer Default' and follow the steps that are presented by the installer.

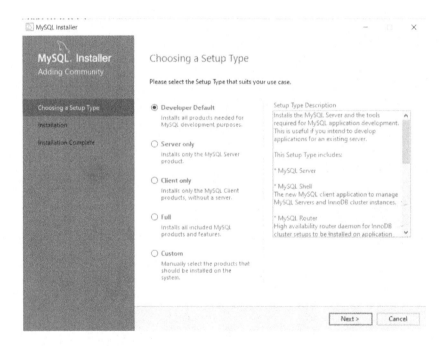

6. After a successful install, the installer will ask you to configure MySQL. Follow the steps until you reach this screen:

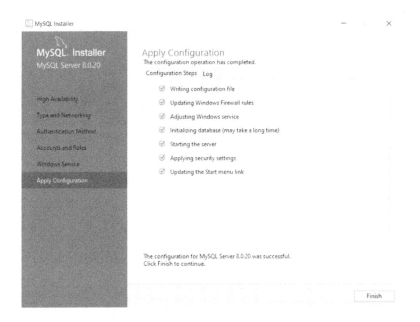

7. Your configuration is complete. Click 'Next' until you reach the final screen of the installer, which should look like this:

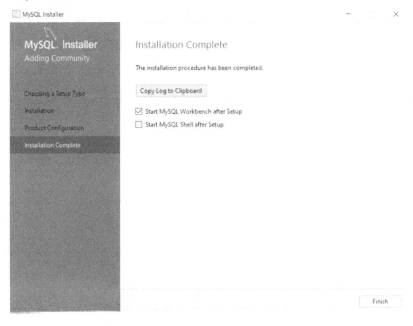

8. Congratulations, you have successfully installed MySQL!

Chapter 3: Establishing a Connection

Let's launch our newly installed MySQL Workbench and connect to a database! After launching the program, you will be greeted by a 'Welcome to MySQL Workbench' message!

Welcome to MySQL Workbench

MySQL Workbench is the official graphical user interface (GUI) tool for MySQL. It allows you to design, create and browse your database schemas, work with database objects and insert data as well as design and run SQL queries to work with stored data. You can also migrate schemas and data from other database vendors to your MySQL database.

Browse Documentation »   Read the Blog »   Discuss on the Forums »

MySQL Connections ⊕ ⊗

Below this greeting is where we want to go next. Click on the small plus icon beside MySQL Connections:

MySQL Connections ⊕ ⊗

This will bring up a panel which will allow us to set up our connection.

The connection name can be whatever you want it to be. For this example, let's just call it 'Local.'

The only other section that needs to be configured is the password. First click the 'Store in Vault' button. This will bring up a pop-up box that will allow you to set your password.

Once you have completed setting your password, click on the 'Test Connection' button. You should receive a confirmation message that you have successfully connected!

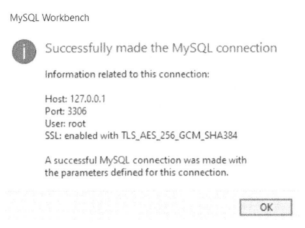

Now let's look at how we can connect to a database using the new connection we have set up. On the home screen you should see the connection created. Click on this connection.

Upon clicking this connection, you should be directed to the main interface we will be using to interact with our currently empty database.

In the MySQL application, creating a database can be done under the 'Schemas' tab. This can be confusing to new users as they will naturally navigate to the Database tab to create a new database.

The first step in creating our new database is to click on the 'Schemas' tab beside Administration on the bottom left of the GUI.

Now, right-click inside of the 'Navigator' panel. You should see an option to 'Create Schema'. Clicking this will allow us to create and configure our database.

You can call your new schema whatever you would like.

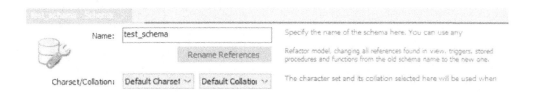

Click 'Apply' to complete the creation of this schema. The final step is to set this as your default schema. Right-click on your newly created schema and select 'Set as Default Schema'.

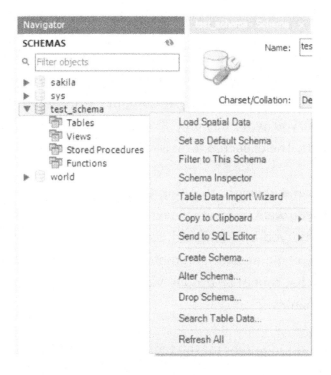

Just like that, you have created a database and you are ready to start writing queries!

Chapter 4: Building up a Database

4.1 - Create Statements

We will be creating a basic table. Remember, a table is a collection of related data held in a table format within a database which will consist of columns and rows. This involves naming the table and defining its columns and each of the column's data types.

The SQL *CREATE TABLE* statement is used to create a new table.

Throughout this book, you will see the word **syntax** when referring to different aspects of SQL, but what does syntax mean? Syntax refers to the spelling and grammar of a programming language. Computers are inflexible machines that understand what you type, but only if you type it in the exact form that the computer expects. The expected form is called the syntax.

CREATE TABLE is the **keyword** that tells the database system what you want to do. In this case, you want to create a new table. What is a keyword? A keyword is a word that is reserved by a program because the word has a special meaning. Keywords can be commands or parameters. Every programming language has a set of keywords that cannot be used as variable names. Keywords are sometimes called reserved names.

The unique name or identifier for the table follows the *CREATE TABLE* statement.

In brackets or parentheses, you must define each column in the table and what sort of data type it is. The syntax becomes clearer with the following example:

```
Query 1  ×

Limit to 1000 rows

1  ● ⊝  CREATE TABLE person_info(
2           PersonID int,
3           FirstName varchar(255),
4           LastName varchar(255),
5           Gender varchar(255),
6           City varchar(255),
7           State varchar(255)|
8        )
```

Let us break down the above SQL query:

First, we define the name of the table by entering text that follows the *CREATE TABLE* keyword. *CREATE TABLE* person_info, creates a table called person_info.

Next, we define our column names. From the example above, the column names are PersonID, FirstName, LastName, Gender, City, and State.

As we define our column names, we simultaneously declare our column data types. This is the text that follows the name of the column.

The syntax is *COLUMN_NAME DATA_TYPE.*

Looking at the example, we can see that FirstName varchar(255), creates a column called FirstName with the data type of varchar(255). Now, you are probably wondering what on earth varchar(255) means; we will review what the different data types mean in the next section.

Finally, to execute your query, click the lightning bolt symbol as shown in the following image:

```
SQL File 5
  📁 💾 ⚡ ⌨ 🔍 ⊙ 🗄 ⊙ ⊗ 🔲  Limit to 1000 rows  ▾  ⚗ 🧹 🔍 🔟 ⇥
  1 ● ⊝ CREATE TABLE person_info(
  2        | Execute the selected portion of the script or everything, if there is no selection |
  3          FirstName varchar(255),
  4          LastName varchar(255),
  5          Gender varchar(255),
  6          City varchar(255),
  7          State varchar(255)
  8      )
```

4.2 - Common Data Types

INT – Stands for Integer, which means whole numbers. For example, 1, 2, 3, 4, 100, 1000, or 4325. All of these are whole numbers, or integers.

DECIMAL (M, N) – The decimal data type will allow you to store decimals. You will notice the letters 'M' and 'N' in the parentheses above. These both represent numbers. The letter 'M' is the total number of digits that you want to store for this number. The letter 'N' is the number of digits that you want to store after the decimal point. When we are working with databases, you have to be very exact about the different information you are trying to store, specifically in the number of digits that you want each decimal number to contain. Suppose that your column is set to be DECIMAL(13,4). This means that the column will have a total size of 13 digits where 4 of these will be used for precision representation, which looks like the following number: 999999999.9999

VARCHAR(255) – This is a string of text. The number denotes the length of the string. *VARCHAR* stands for a variable character. In the parentheses, we enter a number which represents the maximum length that the string of text can be. For example, VARCHAR(5) would allow a string of five characters such as 'hello.'

BLOB – Stands for Binary Large Object, which are typically used to store large data. This is a structure that can store large amounts of binary data. This data type is usually used to store images or files in the database.

DATE – Is a date. We can format a date like YYYY-MM-DD. This would be the year, two-digit month, and the two digit day. For example, '2020-03-30.'

TIMESTAMP – This is used to not only record the date, but also the hour, minute and second. This is usually used for tracking when a certain action is performed. The format of a TIMESTAMP is YYYY-MM-DD HH:MM:SS, which is fixed at 19 characters. For example, '2020-03-30 13:30:15.'

Other Data Types:
Here are the other data types you will encounter when using MySQL. Use this section as a reference when writing your SQL queries. It provides an exhaustive list of the data types available to you in MySQL.

4.3 - Numeric Data Types

The following table shows the summary of numeric types in MySQL:

Numeric Types	Description
TINYINT	A very small integer
SMALLINT	A small integer
MEDIUMINT	A medium-sized integer
INT	A standard integer
BIGINT	A large integer
DECIMAL	A fixed-point number
FLOAT	A single-precision floating point number
DOUBLE	A double-precision floating point number
BIT	A bit field

4.4 - MySQL Boolean Data Types

Note that MySQL does not have the built-in BOOLEAN or BOOL data type. To represent boolean values, MySQL uses the smallest integer type which is TINYINT(1). In other words, BOOLEAN and BOOL are synonyms for TINYINT(1).

4.5 - MySQL String Data Types

In MySQL, a string can hold anything from plain text to binary data such as images or files. Strings can be compared and searched based on pattern matching by using the LIKE operator, regular expressions, or even full-text search. We will explore these actions later in this book.

The following table shows the string data types in MySQL:

STRING DATA TYPES

String Types	Description
CHAR	A fixed-length nonbinary (character) string
VARCHAR	A variable-length non-binary string
BINARY	A fixed-length binary string
VARBINARY	A variable-length binary string
TINYBLOB	A very small BLOB (binary large object)
BLOB	A small BLOB
MEDIUMBLOB	A medium-sized BLOB
LONGBLOB	A large BLOB
TINYTEXT	A very small non-binary string
TEXT	A small non-binary string
MEDIUMTEXT	A medium-sized non-binary string
LONGTEXT	A large non-binary string
ENUM	An enumeration: each column value may be assigned one enumeration member
SET	A set: each column value may be assigned zero or more SET members

4.6 - MySQL Date and Time Data Types

MySQL provides data types for date and time, as well as the combination of date and time. In addition, MySQL supports the timestamp data type for tracking the changes in a row of a table. If you just want to store years without dates and months, you can use the YEAR data type.

The following table illustrates the MySQL date and time data types:

Date and Time Types	Description
DATE	A date value in YYYY-MM-DD format
TIME	A time value in hh:mm:ss format
DATETIME	A date and time value in YYYY-MM-DD hh:mm:ss format
TIMESTAMP	A timestamp value in YYYY-MM-DD hh:mm:ss format
YEAR	A year value in YYYY or YY format

4.7 - MySQL Spatial Data Types

MySQL supports many spatial data types that contain various kinds of geometrical and geographical values as shown in the following table:

Spatial Data Types	Description
GEOMETRY	A spatial value of any type
POINT	A point (a pair of X-Y coordinates)
LINESTRING	A curve (one or more POINT values)
POLYGON	A polygon
GEOMETRYCOLLECTION	A collection of GEOMETRY values
MULTILINESTRING	A collection of LINESTRING values
MULTIPOINT	A collection of POINT values
MULTIPOLYGON	A collection of POLYGON values

4.8 - JSON Data Type

JAVA Script object NOTATION

MySQL supported a native JSON data type since version 5.7.8 that allows you to store and manage JSON documents more effectively. The native JSON data type provides automatic validation of JSON documents and optimal storage format. JSON stands for JavaScript Object Notation. It is a lightweight format for storing and transporting data. JSON is often used when data is sent from a server to a web page.

23

Now that you are equipped with the *CREATE TABLE* keyword and the different data types in MySQL there is nothing stopping you from creating your own custom tables!

> Give It A Try! Try to create another table of your choosing. Determine what data types are appropriate given the chosen columns.

4.9 - Insert Statements – Build Up Your Database

Now that we have created our table successfully, we will learn how we can add data to that table! This is done with the INSERT command.

The INSERT statement allows you to insert one or more rows into a table. The following illustrates the syntax of the INSERT statement:

INSERT INTO table(column_1,column_2, ...column_n)
VALUES (value_1,value_2, ...value_n);

First, specify the table name and a list of comma-separated columns inside parentheses after the INSERT INTO clause.

Next, you put a comma-separated list of values of the corresponding columns inside the parentheses following the VALUES keyword.

The number of columns and values must be the same. In addition, the positions of columns must be corresponding with the positions of their values.

To insert multiple rows into a table using a single INSERT statement, you use the following syntax:

INSERT INTO table(column_1, column_2, ...column_n)
VALUES
    (value_1, value_2, ...value_n),
    (value_3,value_4, ...value_n),
    ...
    (value_n,value_n, ...value_n);

In this syntax, rows are separated by commas in the VALUES clause.

Let's open a new query in MySQL Workbench so we have somewhere to write our new INSERT Statement. To do this, simply click the icon highlighted in the picture below:

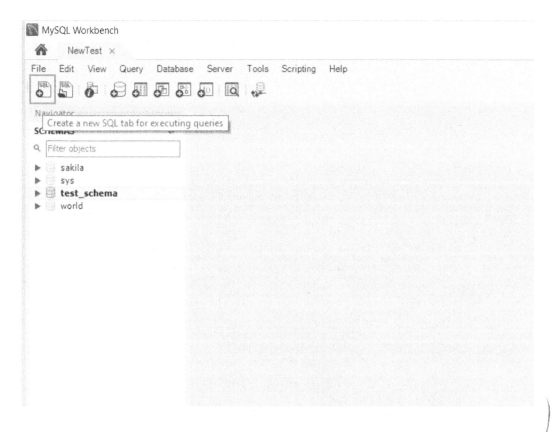

The INSERT statement will not work unless you are inserting the correct data type for each column.

```
INSERT INTO person_info
(PersonID, FirstName, LastName, Gender, City, State)
VALUES
(1, 'Jack', 'Rogers', 'Male', 'Philadelphia', 'PA');
```

Looking at this example, we can see the insertion of correct data types in practice. For PersonID, which is a column with the data type of INT, we enter the numeric value of 1.

The rest of the columns have the VARCHAR data type. This allows text values such as 'Jack' and 'Philadelphia' to be added.

> Give It A Try! Try to add 10 new rows of data to your table to establish a more robust table.

Chapter 5: The SELECT Statement

We are now going to look at the SELECT statement in detail. You will be using the SELECT statement in most, if not all of your SQL queries. The SELECT statement allows you to read data from one or more tables. The simplest way of writing the SELECT statement is to use it with an asterisk (*). When you use an asterisk with the SELECT statement it will retrieve all the columns and rows from the table, or tables you have specified. When developers say they used a 'SELECT ALL' to retrieve the data, they are referring to the use of 'SELECT *'.

SELECT *
FROM table_name

The above SQL query will return all the data from the table 'table_name.'

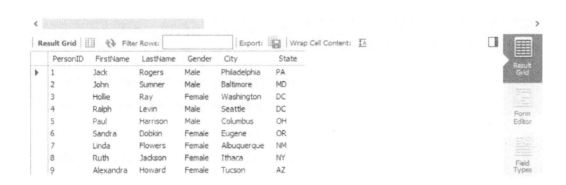

The LIMIT Clause
What is the LIMIT clause?

The limit keyword is used to limit the number of rows returned in a query result. It can be used in conjunction with the SELECT, UPDATE, or DELETE commands.

The syntax for the LIMIT keyword is as follows:

SELECT * FROM table_name(s)
LIMIT [offset,] N;

We will ignore [offset], which is optional, for now.

'SELECT * FROM table_name(s) ' is the SELECT statement containing the fields that we would like to return in our query.

'LIMIT N' is the keyword where N is any number starting from 0, putting 0 as the limit does not return any records in the query. Putting a number, such as 5 will return five records. If the records in the specified table are less than N, then all the records from the queried table are returned in the result set.

Looking at the example above, we can see how LIMIT is used to only retrieve five results from our database.

5.1 - Selecting single columns

While using an asterisk to select all the data from a table is useful; however, it can cause some issues. An overuse of the 'SELECT *' clause can cause the following issues:

- When we write 'SELECT * FROM table_name', the database engine must go into the system tables to read the column metadata in order to materialize the results. This has a small, but measurable performance impact when reading the system tables. If lots of queries use SELECT *, this can cause noticeable locking on the system tables.
- SELECT * returns the columns in the order they were created. This might result in a surprise if a particular order is assumed from output in the past, but the columns have been created in a different order during application upgrades and modifications, which can be reasonably common. Imagine a scenario where one or more columns is appended to the end to avoid rebuilding the whole table; however, in a clean install of the application, those columns might be in a different order. A SELECT * query will, therefore, return the columns in a different order depending on how that table was created and/or modified.
- Do we really need all the columns, all the time? By limiting the columns returned, we can make better use of indexes that consume less space in memory when our queries execute. This is by far the best reason to limit the columns in a SELECT statement. Less memory means fewer storage reads, fewer CPU cycles, and faster queries. Since most databases are accessed over a network, this is another major performance bottleneck we can avoid.

To avoid the issues mentioned above, SQL allows us to specify exact columns we want to retrieve the data for.

```
98  ●    SELECT FirstName, LastName
99       FROM person_info
100
101
```

FirstName	LastName
Jack	Rogers
John	Sumner
Hollie	Ray
Ralph	Levin
Paul	Harrison
Sandra	Dobkin
Linda	Flowers
Ruth	Jackson
Alexandra	Howard

For example, notice with the SQL Query above how we are specifying that we only want to get the data from the FirstName and LastName columns from the person_info table. As you can see in the Results Grid, we only get these two columns, and they are in the same order, as specified here. If we change the order, put 'SELECT LastName, FirstName', and execute the query again we will see the Results Grid display the columns in that order.

5.2 - SELECT DISTINCT

The MySQL SELECT DISTINCT statement is used to retrieve unique rows by removing the duplicate rows from the specified column in the SELECT statement. The default display of MySQL queries is to show all rows, including duplicate rows. The DISTINCT keyword in the SELECT clause is used to eliminate duplicate rows and display a unique list of values.

The basic syntax of the Select Distinct in MySQL can be written as:

SELECT DISTINCT column(s)
FROM table_name

DISTINCT – This keyword returns unique columns.

column(s) – It allows us to choose the number of columns we want to use from the table. It may be one or more.

For example, what if we wanted to check that the information was entered correctly for the Gender column. We would expect to only have two options, Male or Female. We can use the DISTINCT keyword to check that this is indeed the case:

Success! We have validated that there are no errors with the data in our Gender column!

5.3 - SELECT DISTINCT on Multiple Columns

When we use DISTINCT on multiple columns, then the SELECT statement writes the unique combination of multiple columns instead of unique individual records. If you do select more than one column, all columns are combined to create the uniqueness of the row. This is because the DISTINCT option looks for a distinct row, rather than a distinct column.

Viewing Output

You can see the results of your SQL query in the Results Grid. But what if you want to change the order in which those results appear? This can be done by using the ORDER BY keyword.

The main purpose of ORDER BY is to sort the records in your set of results. The syntax for the ORDER BY clause in MySQL is:

SELECT expressions
FROM table(s)
ORDER BY expression [ASC | DESC]

The ORDER BY keyword comes after the FROM keyword. If you use a WHERE condition the ORDER BY keyword must come after WHERE. Beside ORDER BY should be the column you would like to order the result set by. Let's say that we want to order our result set by the LastName. We would use ORDER BY LastName. This displays our results in alphabetical order based on the LastName column.

What if we wanted to display the results in reverse alphabetical order (Z-A)? This is where the ASC and DESC modifiers come into play. ASC stands for ascending, while DESC stands for descending. To use these modifiers, you simply put ASC or DESC following the column name you are ordering by.

For example: ORDER BY LastName DESC

Let's apply this to a practical example:

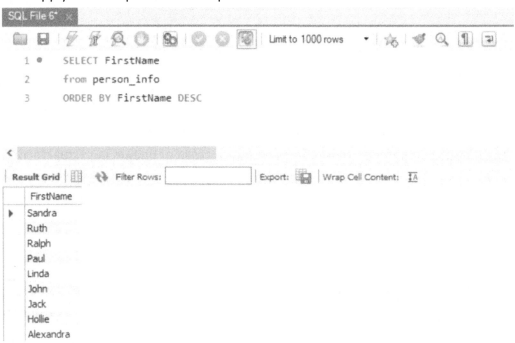

We want to SELECT the first names of people inside of the person_info table. To accomplish this, we simply write SELECT FirstName from person_info. However, we want to display the results in reverse alphabetical order (Z to A). This is where

ORDER BY FirstName DESC comes into effect. The DESC modifier is perfect for this use case.

If you don't use the ASC or DESC modifier, the results will be ordered by ASC (or ascending) order by default.

5.4 - The WHERE Clause

We looked at how to query data from a database using the SELECT statement in the previous tutorial. The SELECT statement returned all of the results from the queried database table. There are, however, times when we want to restrict the query results to a specified condition. The SQL WHERE clause comes in handy in such situations.

The basic syntax for the WHERE clause when used in a SELECT statement is as follows:

```
SELECT *
FROM table_name
WHERE condition
```

'SELECT * FROM table_name' is the standard SELECT statement.

'WHERE' is the keyword that restricts our select query result set and 'condition' is the filter to be applied on the results. The filter can be a range, single value, or sub query.

Let's look at a practical example:

Suppose we want to get the information for females from our person_info table, we would use the following query to achieve this.

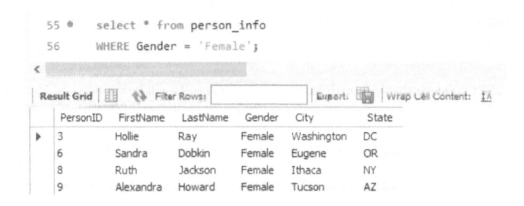

```
55 •     select * from person_info
56       WHERE Gender = 'Female';
```

Result Grid | Filter Rows: | Export: | Wrap Cell Content:

PersonID	FirstName	LastName	Gender	City	State
3	Hollie	Ray	Female	Washington	DC
6	Sandra	Dobkin	Female	Eugene	OR
8	Ruth	Jackson	Female	Ithaca	NY
9	Alexandra	Howard	Female	Tucson	AZ

Now, if we wanted to do the opposite and get the information for males, we can do this in two ways. The first is exactly like above, using the equals operator: **WHERE Gender = 'Male'**

The other way you can achieve this is by using the 'not equals' operator in MySQL, which can be written in two ways: **<>** or **!=**

For example, **WHERE Gender != 'Female'** will return all the records where the gender is not female.

These equals and 'not equals' are called comparison operators, as they compare records and return only the relevant items based on the condition specified in the query. We will briefly look at some other comparison operators that you will find useful.

1. **>** Greater Than

This returns records that have a higher value than the value that follows the 'greater than' symbol.

For example, if we wanted to retrieve a list of employees that were over the age of 50, we would write the following query:

SELECT FirstName, LastName, Age
FROM employees
WHERE Age > 50

2. **>=** Greater Than or Equal

This returns records that have a higher **or equal** value than the value that follows the 'greater than or equals' symbol.

For example, if we wanted to retrieve a list of employees that are 50 years old and older, we would write the following query:

```
SELECT FirstName, LastName, Age
FROM employees
WHERE Age >= 50
```

3. **<** Less Than

This returns records that have a lesser value than the value that follows the 'greater than' symbol.

For example, if we wanted to retrieve a list of employees that were under the age of 50, we would write the following query:

```
SELECT FirstName, LastName, Age
FROM employees
WHERE Age < 50
```

4. **<=** Less Than or Equal

This returns records that have a lesser **or equal** value than the value that follows the 'greater than or equals' symbol.

For example, if we wanted to retrieve a list of employees that were 50 years old and under, we would write the following query:

```
SELECT FirstName, LastName, Age
FROM employees
WHERE Age <= 50
```

We can apply this to our person_info table. What if we wanted to retrieve the records where the PersonID was less than, or equal to five? This is simple:

```
1 •    select * from person_info
2      where PersonID <= 5
```

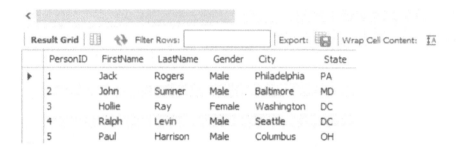

PersonID	FirstName	LastName	Gender	City	State
1	Jack	Rogers	Male	Philadelphia	PA
2	John	Sumner	Male	Baltimore	MD
3	Hollie	Ray	Female	Washington	DC
4	Ralph	Levin	Male	Seattle	DC
5	Paul	Harrison	Male	Columbus	OH

As you can see, it is simply a case of adding PersonID <= 5 to our WHERE clause.

We will now look at using multiple conditions in a query and in doing so will be covering the use of two more operators.

5.5 - AND Operator

The AND operator allows you to retrieve records that fit two or more conditions. This AND example would return all people that are female and live in the state of DC. Since the * is used in the SELECT statement, all fields from the contacts person_info table would appear in the result set.

When combining these conditions, it is important to use parentheses so that the database knows what order to evaluate each condition (just like when you were learning the order of operations in Math class!).

```
55 ●    SELECT * FROM person_info
56      WHERE Gender = 'Female' AND State = 'DC';
57
58
```

Result Grid | Filter Rows: | Export: | Wrap Cell

	PersonID	FirstName	LastName	Gender	City	State
▶	3	Hollie	Ray	Female	Washington	DC

Now let's contrast AND with OR. Look at effect that using the OR keyword has on the same query. Now the SQL query will return all the rows where the Gender is 'Male', or if the state is 'PA.' Look at the example below, the most obvious difference is the first row containing Jack Rogers.

```
1    SELECT * FROM person_info
2    WHERE Gender = 'Male' OR State = 'PA'
3
```

Result Grid | Filter Rows: | Export: | Wrap Cell Content: IA

	PersonID	FirstName	LastName	Gender	City	State
▶	1	Jack	Rogers	Male	Philadelphia	PA
	2	John	Sumner	Male	Baltimore	MD
	4	Ralph	Levin	Male	Seattle	DC
	5	Paul	Harrison	Male	Columbus	OH
	10	Jake	Rogers	Male	Tucson	AZ
	11	Jacob	Rogers	Male	Tucson	AZ

Jack Rogers is 'Male' so even though he didn't fit the first condition (WHERE Gender = 'Female'), he was included in the set of results as his State was 'PA.'

5.6 - HAVING

The HAVING clause is used in the SELECT statement to specify filter conditions for a group of rows or aggregates. The HAVING clause is often combined with the

GROUP BY clause to filter groups based on a specified condition. If the GROUP BY clause is omitted, the HAVING clause behaves similarly to the WHERE clause.

Here is the syntax you will have to follow when using the HAVING clause in your own SQL queries:

```
SELECT
    select_list
FROM
    table_name
WHERE
    search_condition
GROUP BY
    group_by_expression
HAVING
    group_condition;
```

In this syntax, you specify a condition in the HAVING clause. If a row, which is generated by the group by clause, causes the group_condition to evaluate as true, the query will include it in the result set.

Notice that the HAVING clause applies a filter condition to each group of rows, while the WHERE clause applies the filter condition to each individual row.

MySQL evaluates the HAVING clause after the FROM, WHERE, SELECT, and GROUP BY clauses, as well as before ORDER BY, and LIMIT clauses.

Let's say we have an Age column in our person_info table. If we were to execute the following query:

```
SELECT
    Age,
    FirstName,
    LastName
FROM
    person_info
HAVING
```

Age> 30;

This selects the age, first name, and last name of all people over the age of 30.

Let's apply this to a practical example:

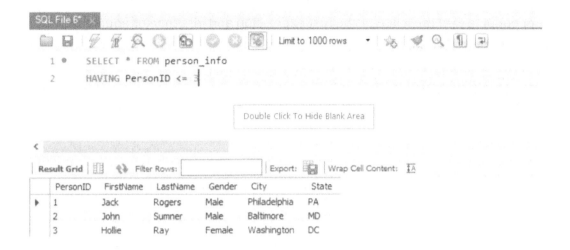

In the example above, we use the HAVING clause to isolate the PersonID values that are less than, or equal to 3. This example can show how similar the functionality between the HAVING clause and the WHERE clause can be.

5.7 - Other Conditional Operators

The BETWEEN Operator
The BETWEEN operator is a logical operator that allows you to specify whether a value is contained within a range or not. The BETWEEN operator is often used in the WHERE clause of the SELECT, UPDATE, and DELETE statements.

The following illustrates the syntax of the BETWEEN operator:

WHERE date [NOT] BETWEEN '2020-03-01' AND '2020-03-30'

The example above will retrieve all records from the table where the date column has a value that lies between the 1st and the 30th of March.

Notice the NOT in square brackets. This means that this is an optional argument that you can include if you wish. If you apply the NOT BETWEEN keyword to the example above the query, it will retrieve all records from table where the date does not lie between the 1st and the 30th of March.

The BETWEEN operator returns true if the value of the expression is greater than or equal to (>=) the value of the first expression and less than or equal to (<=) the value of the second, otherwise, it returns zero.

The NOT BETWEEN returns true if the value of expression is less than (<) the value of the first expression or greater than (>) the value of the value of the second expression, otherwise, it returns 0.

The LIKE condition
The LIKE condition allows you to search for different strings and patterns.
It allows wildcards to be used in the WHERE clause of a SELECT, INSERT, UPDATE, or DELETE statement. This allows you to perform pattern matching. But what is a wildcard?

The first LIKE example below that we will look at involves using the % wildcard (percent sign wildcard). Let's explain how the wildcard % works in the LIKE condition. We want to find all the people who live in states beginning with the letter 'O.' We can achieve this by using pattern matching. SQL pattern matching allows you to search for patterns in data if you do not know the exact word or phrase you are seeking. This kind of SQL query uses wildcard characters to match a pattern, rather than specifying it exactly. For this example, you can use the wildcard 'O%' to match any string beginning with a capital 'O'.

```
55 ●      SELECT * FROM person_info
56        WHERE State LIKE 'O%'
```

<

	PersonID	FirstName	LastName	Gender	City	State
▶	5	Paul	Harrison	Male	Columbus	OH
	6	Sandra	Dobkin	Female	Eugene	OR

You can also use the LIKE condition without wildcards. For example, say we want to find people who lived in the city of Columbus, we could write WHERE City LIKE 'Columbus'. We could also write Where City = 'Columbus'.

What is the difference between using LIKE and equals? Equals, or =, is a comparison operator that operates on numbers and strings. When comparing strings, the comparison operator compares whole strings. LIKE is a string operator that compares character by character.

The IN Operator

We will now learn how to use the IN operator to determine if a specified value matches any value in a list or a subquery. The IN operator has the following syntax:

SELECT column_name(s)
FROM table_name
WHERE column_name IN (value_1, value_2, ... value_n);

Let's apply this syntax to a practical example.

```
55 ●     SELECT * FROM person_info
56       WHERE State IN ('PA','MD','DC')
57
```

PersonID	FirstName	LastName	Gender	City	State
1	Jack	Rogers	Male	Philadelphia	PA
2	John	Sumner	Male	Baltimore	MD
3	Hollie	Ray	Female	Washington	DC

This IN condition example would return all rows from the person_info table where the State is either 'PA', 'MD 'or 'DC.' Since the * is used in the SELECT, all fields from the person_info table would appear in the result set.

The NOT condition

The NOT condition requires that the opposite of the condition be met for the record to be included in the result set.

For example, the NOT condition can be combined with the IN condition, as we have previously mentioned.

SELECT *
FROM person_info
WHERE State NOT IN ('PA','MD','DC')

This example would return all rows from the contacts table where the state is not 'PA, 'MD, or 'DC.' Sometimes, it is more efficient to list the values that you do not want, as opposed to the values that you do want.

IS NULL

You may be wondering what NULL means. In a database, zero is a value. The value NULL means that no value exists. When used as a value, NULL is not a memory location. Only pointers hold memory locations. Without a NULL character, a string would not correctly terminate, which would cause problems.

The IS NULL Condition is used to test for a NULL value in a SELECT, INSERT, UPDATE, or DELETE statement. The syntax for the IS NULL Condition in MySQL is:

WHERE expression IS NULL

Let's look at an example of how to use IS NULL in a SELECT statement:

SELECT *
FROM person_info
WHERE FirstName IS NULL

This MySQL IS NULL example will return all records from the contacts table where the FirstName contains a NULL value.

In simple terms, NULL is simply a place holder for data that does not exist. When performing insert operations on tables, there will be times when some field values will not be available. To meet the requirements of true relational DBMSs, MySQL uses NULL as the place holder for the values that have not been submitted.

Let's summarize the basics for NULL, some of the rules, and properties that you must remember.

1. NULL is not a data type, this means it is not recognized as an INT, DateTime, or any other defined data type.
2. Arithmetic operations involving NULL always return NULL. For example, NULL + 100 = NULL.
3. All aggregate functions affect only rows that do not have NULL values.
4. The NOT logical operator is used to test for Boolean conditions and returns true if the condition is false. The NOT operator returns false if the condition being tested is true.

Why use NOT NULL?
There will be cases when we will have to perform computations on a query result set and return the values. Performing any arithmetic operations on columns that

have the NULL value returns NULL results. To avoid such situations, we can make use of the NOT NULL clause to limit the results on which our data operates.

Chapter 6: Using Regular Expressions

We have covered the LIKE operator before, it is in fact, what is called a regular expression! The LIKE operator is a logical operator that tests whether a string contains a specified pattern or not. The LIKE operator is used in the WHERE clause of the SELECT, DELETE, and UPDATE statements to filter data based on patterns.

Here is the syntax of the LIKE operator:
- MySQL provides two wildcard characters for constructing patterns: percentage % and underscore _ .
- The percentage (%) wildcard matches any string of zero or more characters.
- The underscore (_) wildcard matches any single character.

For example, 'H%' matches any string starts with the character 'H' such as Hat and Hen. Then 'He_' matches any string starts with 'He' and is followed by any character such as Hen or Hep but would not match with Hello or Help. While 'He___' (three underscores) would match with Hello but not Hen, Hep, or Help.

If you know the string you are looking for is embedded inside in the middle of a string, you can use the percentage (%) wildcard at the beginning and the end of the pattern.

For example, to find all employees whose last names contain 'ac', you use the following query with the pattern %ac%

```
SELECT
    FirstName,
    LastName
FROM
    person_info
WHERE
    LastName LIKE '%ac%';
```

LIKE Operator with prefix and suffix patterns
Using MySQL LIKE with underscore(_) wildcard.

To find employees whose first names start with T, end with M, and contain any single character between, for example, Tom and Tim, you can use the underscore (_) wildcard to construct the pattern as follows:

```
SELECT
    FirstName,
    LastName
FROM
    person_info
WHERE
    FirstName LIKE 'T_m';
```

MySQL LIKE operator with the ESCAPE clause
Sometimes the pattern which you want to match contains a wildcard character. What if you have a column with the data type VARCHAR that contains data such as '10%,' or perhaps our data contains underscores such as '_10'? In this case, you can use the ESCAPE clause to specify the escape character, so that MySQL will interpret the wildcard character as a literal character. I know this sounds confusing, but it is quite simple in practice. By default, we use the backslash (\ ) character as our escape character.

For example, let's say we have a table of products. If you want to find products whose product codes contain the string '_10,' you can use the pattern %_10% as shown in the following query:

```
SELECT
    ProductCode,
    ProductName
FROM
    products_table
WHERE
    ProductCode LIKE '%\_10%';
```

This covers most situations where you may need to use the LIKE operator. Now let's look at regular expressions in more detail.

Regular expressions help search data that matches complex criteria. We have previously looked at wildcards and how they allow us to use pattern matching to retrieve the result set we want. You may be asking what the point is to learning regular expressions when you can get similar results by using wildcards. The main reason is that when compared to wildcards, regular expressions allow us to search our database using pattern matching with an even more complex criterion. Regular expressions are more powerful and robust than just using wildcards.

When using regular expressions, we make use of metacharacters to correctly implement pattern matching. The first metacharacter we will look at in detail is the caret metacharacter, which is this character: ^.

This character matches the start of the string to whatever text follows the ^ symbol. Let's now look at a practical example:

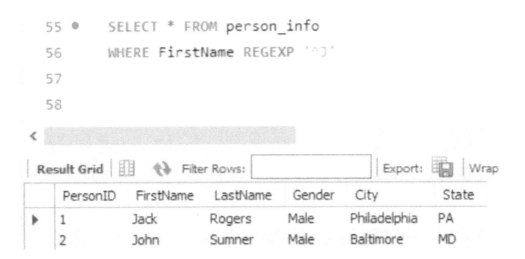

'^J' the caret (^) makes this query search for first names starting with the letter J. Notice how it returns the results Jack and John, which is the result set we expect.

The next metacharacter to highlight is the dollar sign or $ symbol. This symbol allows you to match the end of a string. Let's look at the example below. We want to find last names that end with the letter 'S'. The $ metacharacter allows us to do this by simply entering 'S$.'

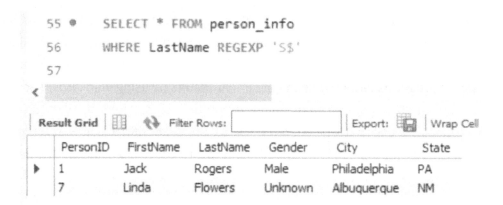

Notice how the LastName column shows the results that we expect. Both 'Rogers' and 'Flowers' end with the letter 'S.'

The final metacharacter to be discussed in detail is the **dot (.)** metacharacter. This is used to match any single character. In other words, you can search for data that contains a certain character. For example, if we wanted to search for people who had a last name that contained the letter 'A,' we would write the following query:

Take a closer look at the 'LastName' column returned by this SQL query. Each surname contains the letter 'A.' This is exactly what we hoped to achieve.

6.1 - Regular Expression Metacharacter Cheat Sheet

What we looked at in the above example is the simplest form of a regular expression. Let's now look at more advanced regular expression pattern matches. Suppose we want to search for movie titles that start with the pattern 'code' only using a regular expression, how would we do this? The answer is metacharacters. They allow us to fine tune our pattern search results by using regular expressions.

Char	Description	Example
*	The **asterisk (*)** metacharacter is used to match zero (0) or more instances of the strings preceding it	SELECT * FROM person_info WHERE FirstName REGEXP 'oh*', will give all person_info containing characters 'oh.' In this case, John.
+	The **plus (+)** metacharacter is used to match one or more instances of strings preceding it.	SELECT * FROM person_info WHERE FirstName REGEXP 'Ral+'; will give all the first names containing characters 'Ral.' In this case, Ralph.
?	The **question(?)** metacharacter is used to match zero (0) or one instances of the strings preceding it.	SELECT * FROM person_info WHERE FirstName REGEXP 'Al?'; will give all the first names containing string containing 'Al.' In this case, 'Alexandra' and 'Alan'
.	The **dot (.)** metacharacter is used to match any single character in exception of a new line.	SELECT * FROM person_info WHERE FirstName REGEXP 'u.'; will give all the first names containing the letter 'u' followed by any single character. For example, Paul and Ruth.
[abc]	The **charlist [abc]** is used to match any of the enclosed characters.	SELECT * FROM person_info WHERE FirstName REGEXP '[aeiou]'; will give all the names containing any single character in 'aeiou.' In this case, all the records should be returned.

[^abc]	The **charlist [^abc]** is used to match any characters excluding the ones enclosed.	SELECT * FROM person_info WHERE FirstName REGEXP '^[^au]'; will give all the first names containing characters other than the ones in 'au.' In this case it will return John and Hollie.
[A-Z]	The **[A-Z]** is used to match any upper-case letter.	SELECT * FROM person_info WHERE FirstName REGEXP '[A-Z]'; will give all the people that have a first name containing any character from A to Z.
[a-z]	The **[a-z]** is used to match any lower-case letter.	SELECT * FROM person_info WHERE FirstName REGEXP '[a-z]', will give all the people that have first name containing any character from a to z.
[0-9]	The **[0-9]** is used to match any digit from 0 through to 9.	SELECT * FROM person_info WHERE PersonID REGEXP '[0-9]' will give all the people that have PersonID's containing characters '[0-9].'
^	The **caret (^)** is used to start the match at beginning.	SELECT * FROM person_info WHERE FirstName REGEXP '^[Hol]', gives all the people with first names starting with 'Hol.' In this case Hollie should be shown.
|	The **vertical bar (|)** is used to isolate alternatives.	SELECT * FROM person_info WHERE FirstName REGEXP '^[Hol]|^[Alex]'; gives all the people that have a first name starting with any of the characters in 'Hol' or 'Alex.' In this case, Hollie and Alexandra will be shown.
[[:<:]]	The **[[:<:]]** matches the beginning of words.	SELECT * FROM person_info WHERE FirstName REGEXP '[[:<:]]Lin', gives all the people with first names

		starting with the characters 'Lin.' In this case it should return Linda.
[[:>:]]	The **[[:>:]]** matches the end of words.	SELECT * FROM person_info WHERE FirstName REGEXP 'ack[[:>:]]', gives all the people with first names ending with the characters 'ack.' In this case Jack should be shown.
[:class:]	The **[:class:]** matches a character class i.e. [:alpha:] to match letters, [:space:] to match white space, [:punct:] is match punctuations and [:upper:] for upper class letters.	SELECT * FROM person_info WHERE FirstName REGEXP '[:alpha:]'; gives all the people with first names that only contain letters. All names should be shown here, as they should not contain numerical values or whitespace.

6.2 - Regular Expression Summary

- Regular expressions provide a powerful and flexible pattern matching that can help us implement power search utilities for our database systems.
- REGEXP is the operator used when performing regular expression pattern matches.
- Regular expressions support a number of metacharacters, which allow for more flexibility and control when performing pattern matches.
- The backslash is used as an escape character in regular expressions. It's only considered in the pattern match if double backslashes are used. If we want to use it as part of the pattern in a regular expression, we should use double backslashes (\\).
- Regular expressions are not case sensitive.

Give It A Try! Determine all people who have an 'A' in both their last name and their hometown, or have a first name ending in 'A.'

Chapter 7: Table Joins

In this lesson, we will be using techniques that utilize multiple tables within a database. The following tables will need to be created to work with table joins.

> Give It A Try! Create two additional tables that could be related to the person_info table.
>
> Make the first called 'city_info' that contains a city ID (incrementing from 1), the city name, state abbreviation, and the population of the city. Use 5 of the cities included in the original table displayed previously and add 3 additional cities not in the original table.
>
> Make the second called 'ssn_keys', which contains the PersonID from the original table and a 9-digit number. Include 5 rows with PersonIDs from the original table. Make the SSN a varchar(255), so that leading zeros are not dropped.

7.1 - What are JOINs?

JOINs help retrieve data from two or more database tables. The tables are mutually related using primary and foreign keys. JOIN is the most misunderstood topic among SQL learners. There are multiple types of JOINs we must learn about to gain a complete understanding of the usefulness and power of the JOIN command.

7.2 - INNER JOIN

The INNER JOIN is used to return rows from both tables that satisfy the given condition.

The INNER JOIN matches each row in one table with every row in other tables and allows you to query rows that contain columns from both tables.

The INNER JOIN is an optional clause of the SELECT statement. It appears immediately after the FROM clause. Here is the syntax of the INNER JOIN clause:

```
SELECT
    select_list
FROM table_1
INNER JOIN table_2 ON join_condition_1
INNER JOIN table_3 ON join_condition_2
```

In this syntax:

Specify the main table that appears in the FROM clause (table_1).

Next, specify the table that will be joined with the main table, which appears in the INNER JOIN clause (table_2, table_3,…).

Third, specify a JOIN condition after the ON keyword of the INNER JOIN clause. The JOIN condition specifies the rule for matching rows between the main table and the table appeared in the INNER JOIN clause.

Assuming that you want to join two tables table_1 and table_2.

If rows from both tables cause the JOIN condition to evaluate to TRUE, the INNER JOIN creates a new row whose columns contain all columns of rows from the tables and includes this new row in the result set. Otherwise, the INNER JOIN just ignores the rows.

In case no row between tables causes the JOIN condition to evaluate to TRUE, the INNER JOIN returns an empty result set. This logic is also applied when you join more than 2 tables.

Let's apply this to a practical example.

```
1  •    SELECT ci.City, ci.State, ci.Population FROM
2       person_info as pi
3       INNER JOIN
4       city_info as ci
5       ON pi.City = ci.City
6       AND pi.State = ci.State
7
```

Result Grid | Filter Rows: | Export: | Wrap Cell Content:

City	State	Population
▶ Philadelphia	PA	1581000
Baltimore	MD	345043
Columbus	OH	323443
Eugene	OR	168916
Ithaca	NY	31006
Tucson	AZ	535677
Tucson	AZ	535677
Tucson	AZ	535677
Topeka	KS	126587

Looking at the SELECT clause, we can see that we want to retrieve the City, State, and Population data.

Now look at the FROM keyword, it's referencing our person_info table.
Next look at the INNER JOIN, it's joining one table, city_info.
We are joining this city_info table on two conditions, the City, and the State. The city_info table data will only be included where the City can be found in both tables, and where the values equal. The same goes for State and the city_info table. State data will only be included where the State can be found in both tables, and where the values are equal.

You may have noticed the use of the 'as' in the SQL query above. In SQL, this is called an **Alias.**

7.3 - MySQL Alias for Columns

Sometimes, column names can be quite technical and not very understandable. This can make the query's output very difficult to understand at first glance. To give a column a descriptive name, you can use a column alias.

The following statement illustrates how to use the column alias:

SELECT
    [column_1] AS descriptive_name
FROM table_name;

To assign an alias to a column, you use the AS keyword followed by the alias. If the alias contains spaces, you must quote it as the following:

SELECT
    [column_1 | expression] AS 'descriptive with space'
FROM
    table_name;

Because the AS keyword is optional, you can omit it in the statement. Note that you can also give an expression an alias.

Apply our new INNER JOIN and Alias knowledge to the exercise below!

Give It A Try! Get the city names, state names, and population of all cities from which there is a person in the database.

7.4 - LEFT JOIN

The LEFT JOIN allows you to query data from two or more tables. Like the INNER JOIN clause, the LEFT JOIN is an optional clause of the SELECT statement, which appears immediately after the FROM clause. But what is the key difference between LEFT JOIN and INNER JOIN?

Use a LEFT JOIN when you want all the results that are in the first table listed. Use a INNER JOIN when you want some results from the second table if they match the condition.

Suppose that you want to join two tables table_1 and table_2.

The following statement shows how to use the LEFT JOIN clause to join the two tables:

SELECT

```
    select_list
FROM
    table_1
LEFT JOIN table_2 ON
    join_condition
```

When you use the LEFT JOIN clause, the concepts of the left table and the right table are introduced.

In the above syntax, table_1 is the left table and table_2 is the right table.
The LEFT JOIN clause selects data starting from the left table (table_1). It matches each row from the left table (table_1) with every row from the right table (table_2) based on the join_condition.

If the rows from both tables causes the join condition to be evaluated as TRUE, the LEFT JOIN combine columns of rows from both tables to a new row and includes this new row in the result rows.
In case the row from the left table (table_1) does not match with any row from the right table(table_2), the LEFT JOIN still combines columns of rows from both tables into a new row and includes the new row in the result rows. However, it uses NULL for all the columns of the row from the right table.

In other words, LEFT JOIN returns all rows from the left table regardless of whether a row from the left table has a matching row from the right table or not. If there is no match, the columns of the row from the right table will contain NULL.

Let's apply this to a practical example:

```
111 •    SELECT pi.City, pi.State, ci.Population FROM
112      person_info as pi
113      LEFT JOIN
114      city_info as ci
115      ON pi.City = ci.City
116      AND pi.State = ci.State
117
118
```

City	State	Population
Philadelphia	PA	1581000
Topeka	KS	126587
Eugene	OR	168916
Tucson	AZ	535677
Ithaca	NY	31006
Baltimore	MD	NULL
Washington	DC	NULL
Seattle	WA	NULL
Columbus	OH	NULL

Look at the SELECT clause, we want to retrieve the City and State data from person_info, along with the Population data from city_info.

Now let's look at the LEFT JOIN and its conditions. We are joining the city_info table on the City and the State, like the example that was previously shown for INNER JOIN. However, the output is drastically different. The use of LEFT JOIN means we show all the cities and states from our left table (person_info), even if there is no matching record in our right table (city_info). Where no match can be found, the Results Grid shows a NULL value in the population column.

> Give It A Try! List all the cities and states people in the database, and the population of the city if available.

7.5 - RIGHT JOIN

RIGHT JOIN is like LEFT JOIN, except that the treatment of the joined tables is reversed. It essentially performs the opposite action to the LEFT JOIN.

Here is the syntax of the RIGHT JOIN of two tables table_1 and table_2:

```
SELECT
    select_list
FROM table_1
RIGHT JOIN table_2 ON
    join_condition;
```

In this syntax:

table_1 is the left table and table_2 is the right table.
join_condition specifies the rule for matching rows in both tables.

The RIGHT JOIN starts selecting data from the right table (table_2). It matches each row from the right table with every row from the left table. If both rows cause the join condition to be evaluated as TRUE, it combines the columns into a new row and includes this new row in the result set.

If a row from the right table does not have a matching row from the left table, it combines columns of rows from the right table with NULL values for all the columns of the right table into a new row and includes this row in the result set. In other words, the RIGHT JOIN returns all rows from the right table regardless of having matching rows from the left table or not.

It's important to emphasize that RIGHT JOIN and LEFT JOIN clauses are functionally equivalent, and they can replace each other as long as the table order is reversed.

Note that the RIGHT OUTER JOIN is a synonym for RIGHT JOIN.

Now let's look at a practical example:

```
1 ●   SELECT pi.City, pi.State, ci.Population
2     FROM person_info as pi
3     RIGHT JOIN
4     city_info as ci
5     ON pi.City = ci.City
6     AND pi.State = ci.State
```

Look at the SELECT clause, we want to retrieve the City and State data from person_info, along with the Population data from city_info.

Now let's look at the RIGHT JOIN and its conditions. We are joining the city_info table on the City and the State, like the example that was previously shown for LEFT JOIN. However, the output will be different. The use of RIGHT JOIN means we show all the cities and states from our right table (city_info), even if there is no matching record in our left table (person_info). Where no match can be found, the Results Grid shows a NULL value in the population column.

> Give It A Try! List all the cities in the city_info table and what PersonIDs are from that city, if any.

7.6 - CROSS JOIN

Another type of JOIN that you may find useful when writing your queries is the CROSS JOIN.

The CROSS JOIN clause returns the Cartesian product of rows from the joined tables.

In the real world, CROSS JOIN is used when you need to find out all the possibilities of combining two tables where the result set includes every row from each contributing table.

CROSS JOIN (without a WHERE clause or ON clause in join condition) produces a result set where its size is the number of rows in the first table multiplying the number of rows in the second table. This type of result is called Cartesian Product of two tables (table 1 x table 2). Look at the example below to get a clearer understanding of how cross joins work.

Table 1

A
B
C

Table 2

1
2
3

After performing a CROSS JOIN, the result set can appear as follows:

Result Set

1	A
1	B
1	C
2	A
2	B
2	C
3	A
3	B
3	C

The syntax for using CROSS JOIN is as follows:

SELECT * FROM table_1
CROSS JOIN table_2;

Notice how CROSS JOIN does not use ON or USING when it is being declared. This is different from the JOINs we have previously reviewed.

If you decide to insert a WHERE clause, the CROSS JOIN behaves like the INNER JOIN clause as shown in the following query:

```
SELECT * FROM table_1
CROSS JOIN table_2
WHERE table_1.id = table_2.id;
```

7.7 - UNION

There is another popular method to retrieve data from multiple tables. This is the UNION operator.

The MySQL UNION operator is used to combine the result sets of two or more SELECT statements. It removes duplicate rows between the various SELECT statements. Each SELECT statement within the UNION operator must have the same number of fields in the result sets with similar data types. You cannot select three columns in your first SELECT statement, select two columns in your second SELECT statement, and hope to combine the two result sets using the UNION operator.

The syntax that must be followed when using the UNION operator is explained below:

```
SELECT column_1, column_2, ...column_n
FROM table(s)
UNION [DISTINCT]
SELECT column_1, column_2, ...column_n
FROM table(s)
```

SELECT column_1, column_2, ...column_n – these are the columns or calculations that you wish to retrieve from the database.

table(s) – these are the tables you are pulling the data from. There must be at least one table listed in the FROM clause.

DISTINCT – This is optional and can be used in addition with UNION operator. This DISTINCT keyword removes duplicates from the result set, but the inclusion of the DISTINCT modifier has no impact on the result set of the UNION operator because, by default, the UNION operator already removes duplicates.

When using the UNION operator remember the following:

1. There must be the same number of expressions in both SELECT statements.
2. Since the UNION operator by default removes all duplicate rows from the result set, providing the UNION DISTINCT modifier has no effect on the results.
3. The column names from the first SELECT statement in the UNION operator are used as the column names for the result set.

The following is an example of the MySQL UNION operator that returns one field from multiple SELECT statements (and both fields have the same data type):

```
SELECT PersonID
FROM person_info
UNION
SELECT PersonID
FROM ssn_keys;
```

In this MySQL UNION operator example, if a PersonID appeared in both the person_info and ssn_keys table, it would appear once in your result set. The MySQL UNION operator removes duplicates. If you do not wish to remove duplicates, you can use the MySQL UNION ALL operator.

Example – Using ORDER BY

The MySQL UNION operator can use the ORDER BY clause to order the results of the query.

The UNION ALL operator is used to combine the result sets of 2 or more SELECT statements. It returns all rows from the query and it does not remove duplicate rows between the various SELECT statements. Each SELECT statement within the MySQL UNION ALL operator must have the same number of fields in the result sets with similar data types.

Chapter 8: Setting Primary and Foreign Keys

8.1 - What is a primary key in MySQL?

In MySQL, a primary key is a field or combination of fields that uniquely defines a record. None of the fields that are part of the primary key can contain a NULL value. A table can only have one primary key.

A primary key is created using either a CREATE TABLE statement or an ALTER TABLE statement. You use the ALTER TABLE statement in MySQL to drop, disable, or enable a primary key.

A primary key is a column or a set of columns that uniquely identifies each row in the table.

The primary key follows these rules:
1. A primary key must contain unique values. If the primary key consists of multiple columns, the combination of values in these columns must be unique.
2. A primary key column cannot have NULL values. Any attempt to insert or update NULL to primary key columns will result in an error. Note that MySQL implicitly adds a NOT NULL constraint to primary key columns.
3. A table can have one, and only one, primary key.

Because MySQL works faster with integers, the data type of the primary key column should be the integer. For example, data types such as INT and BIGINT. You should ensure sure that value ranges of the integer type for the primary key are sufficient for storing all possible rows that the table may have. If the table you are creating will have a lot of records, the INT data type might not be the correct choice.

Look at the table below:

Type	Storage (Bytes)	Minimum Value Signed	Minimum Value Unsigned	Maximum Value Signed	Maximum Value Unsigned
TINYINT	1	-128	0	127	255
SMALLINT	2	-32768	0	32767	65535
MEDIUMINT	3	-8388608	0	8388607	16777215
INT	4	-2147483648	0	2147483647	4294967295
BIGINT	8	-2^{63}	0	$2^{63}-1$	$2^{64}-1$

Look at the minimum and maximum value signed columns. If you set the primary key to be a TINY INT, that has a maximum value of 127, you will encounter an error when there is a 128th record inserted into the table. For primary keys, bigger is better.

A primary key column often has the AUTO_INCREMENT attribute that automatically generates a sequential integer whenever you insert a new row into the table. Let's say we have a column called PersonID, which uniquely identifies a person in our table. With AUTO_INCREMENT, every time a new person is inserted into our table, they will be automatically assigned a new PersonID.

When you define a primary key for a table, MySQL automatically creates an **index** called PRIMARY.

8.2 - What is an index?

Indexes are used to find rows with specific column values quickly. Without an index, MySQL must begin with the first row and then read through the entire table to find the relevant rows. The larger the table, the more this costs. If the table has an index for the columns in question, MySQL can quickly determine the position to seek to in the middle of the data file without having review all data. This is much faster than reading every row sequentially.

MySQL uses indexes for the following operations:

1. To find the rows matching a WHERE clause quickly.

2. To eliminate rows from consideration. If there is a choice between multiple indexes, MySQL normally uses the index that finds the smallest number of rows (the most selective index).

3. To retrieve rows from other tables when performing joins. MySQL can use indexes on columns more efficiently if they are declared as the same type and size. In this context, VARCHAR and CHAR are considered the same if they are declared as the same size. For example, VARCHAR(10) and CHAR(10) are the same size, but VARCHAR(10) and CHAR(15) are not.

4. For comparisons between string columns.

Indexes are less important for queries on small tables, or big tables where report queries process most or all the rows. When a query needs to access most of the rows, reading sequentially is faster than working through an index.

With the basics of primary keys and indexing explained, it is time for you to learn how to use primary keys effectively.

The main purpose of a primary key is to identify the uniqueness of a row, whereas a unique key is to prevent the duplicates. The following are the main differences between a primary key and unique key. The primary key enforces the entity integrity of the table. All columns defined must be defined as NOT NULL.

8.3 - Establishing Primary Keys

A primary key is created at the same time you create the table. You specify what column will be the primary key when you use the CREATE TABLE statement.

The syntax to create a primary key using the CREATE TABLE statement in MySQL is:

```
CREATE TABLE table_name
(
   column_1 column_data_type PRIMARY KEY,
   column_2 column_data_type,
   ...
   column_n
);
```

In this syntax:

table_name is the name of the table that you want to create.

Next, column_1, column_2 are the names of the columns you are creating.

The column_data_type represents the data types for each column. For example, INT, VARCHAR, etc.

Finally comes the PRIMARY KEY constraint. Place this after the data type for the column.

Let's apply the syntax for CREATE TABLE to a practical example:

```
CREATE TABLE person_info(
    PersonID int PRIMARY KEY,
    FirstName varchar(255),
    LastName varchar(255),
    Gender varchar(255),
    City varchar(255),
    State varchar(255)
);
```

In the query above, we are creating a table called person_info. Look at the first column we are creating. It is clear that PersonID, with the data type INT, is being specified as our PRIMARY KEY.

What if we wanted to create a primary key consisting of two columns?

Let's imagine we have the following:

```
CREATE TABLE person_info (
        PersonID int,
        Age int,
        FirstName varchar(255),
        LastName varchar(255),
        PRIMARY KEY(PersonID, Age)
    )
```

As you can see, creating primary keys is quite simple when you do so as you are creating the table using the CREATE TABLE statement. However, there are situations where you may want to add a primary key to a table after it has already been created. For this, we use the ALTER TABLE statement.

8.4 - Using Alter Table Statement for Primary Keys

Syntax
The syntax to create a primary key using the ALTER TABLE statement in MySQL is simply:

ALTER TABLE table_name
    ADD PRIMARY KEY (column1, column2, ... column_n)

The name of the table to modify is: table_name
constraint_name
The columns (column1, column2, ... column_n) that make up the primary key are specified in brackets after the ADD PRIMARY KEY statement.

Let's look at a practical example of how to create a primary key using the ALTER TABLE statement in MySQL.

```
ALTER TABLE person_info
ADD PRIMARY KEY (PersonID);
```

We have a table that has already been created and called person_info. If we want to add a primary key to the PersonID column of this table, we simply use: ADD PRIMARY KEY (PersonID);

That's all there is to it!

What if we want to delete or remove a primary key from a table?
To accomplish this, we will use of the DROP keyword in MySQL. It performs exactly as it sounds, essentially removing, or dropping, the primary key from the table.

The syntax to drop a primary key in MySQL is:

```
ALTER TABLE table_name
    DROP PRIMARY KEY;
```

Where table_name is the name of the table.

We do not need to specify the name of the primary key as there can only be one on a table.

8.5 - Establishing Composite Primary Keys

Composite key, or composite primary key, refers to cases where more than one column is used to specify the primary key of a table. In such cases, all foreign keys will also need to include all the columns in the composite key. Note that the columns that make up a composite key can be of different data types.

8.6 - What is a Foreign Key

A foreign key is a column or group of columns in a table that links to a column or group of columns in another table. The foreign key places constraints on data in the related tables, which allows MySQL to maintain referential integrity. Referential integrity refers to the accuracy and consistency of data within a relationship. In relationships, data is linked between two or more tables. This is achieved by having the foreign key reference a primary key value.

Typically, the foreign key columns of the child table often refer to the primary key columns of the parent table. A table can have more than one foreign key where each foreign key references to a primary key of the different parent tables.

Once a foreign key constraint is in place, the foreign key columns from the child table must have the corresponding row in the parent key columns of the parent table or values in these foreign key columns must be NULL.

8.7 - Why do we need Foreign Keys?

The FOREIGN KEY constraint is used to prevent actions that would destroy links between tables. The FOREIGN KEY constraint also prevents invalid data from being inserted into the foreign key column, because it must be one of the values contained in the table it points to.

Here is the basic syntax of defining a foreign key constraint in the CREATE TABLE or ALTER TABLE statement:

```
FOREIGN KEY [foreign_key_name] (column_name, ...)
REFERENCES parent_table(colunm_name,...)
[ON DELETE reference_option] -- Optional
[ON UPDATE reference_option] -- Optional
```

In this syntax:
First, specify a list of comma-separated foreign key columns after the FOREIGN KEY keywords. The foreign key name is also optional and is generated automatically if you skip it.

Second, specify the parent table followed by a list of comma-separated columns to which the foreign key columns reference.

Third, you can specify how foreign key maintains the referential integrity between the child and parent tables by using the ON DELETE and ON UPDATE clauses. The reference_option determines the action which MySQL will take when values in the parent key columns are deleted (ON DELETE) or updated (ON UPDATE).

MySQL has five reference options: CASCADE, SET NULL, NO ACTION, RESTRICT, and SET DEFAULT.

1. CASCADE: if a row from the parent table is deleted or updated, the values of the matching rows in the child table are automatically deleted or updated.
2. SET NULL: if a row from the parent table is deleted or updated, the values of the foreign key column (or columns) in the child table are set to NULL.
3. RESTRICT: if a row from the parent table has a matching row in the child table, MySQL rejects deleting or updating rows in the parent table.
4. NO ACTION: is the same as RESTRICT.
5. SET DEFAULT: is recognized by the MySQL parser. However, this action is rejected by both InnoDB and NDB tables.

In fact, MySQL fully supports three actions: RESTRICT, CASCADE and SET NULL.

If you don't specify the ON DELETE and ON UPDATE clause, the default action is RESTRICT.

However this can differ based the variety of SQL you are currently using. For example, SQL Server defaults to CASCADE, while both MySQL and Oracle default to NO ACTION.

Let's apply this new knowledge by looking at a practical example. We want to create a foreign key to create a link between our person_info table, and our social security number table, ssn_keys. This way, if we try to delete a social security number from the ssn_keys table, MySQL will restrict us from doing so, as this table is linked person_info.

```
CREATE TABLE ssn_keys(
    PersonID int,
    SSN varchar(255),
    FOREIGN KEY (PersonID) REFERENCES person_info(PersonID)
);
```

When creating our ssn_keys table you can see how we are linking the PersonID of ssn_keys to the PersonID column of person_info:

FOREIGN KEY (PersonID) REFERENCES person_info(PersonID)

The example above shows how we can create a foreign key when using the CREATE TABLE statement. Now let's look at how we can accomplish the same when the table has already been created. We can achieve this by using the ALTER TABLE statement. Let's look at the practical example below:

```
ALTER TABLE ssn_keys
ADD FOREIGN KEY (PersonID) REFERENCES person_info(PersonID);
```

For this example, let's assume that the ssn_keys already exists with the following columns:

```
PersonID int,
SSN varchar(255)
```

To create a connection between the tables we simply write:
ALTER TABLE ssn_keys
ADD FOREIGN KEY (PersonID) REFERENCES person_info(PersonID);

This creates a link between the PersonID columns of both tables.

8.8 - TEMPORARY Tables

In MySQL, a temporary table is a special type of table that allows you to store a temporary result set, which you can reuse several times in a single session.

A temporary table is very useful when it's impossible or expensive to query data that requires a single SELECT statement in conjunction with JOIN clauses. In this case, you can use a temporary table to store the immediate result and use another query to process it.

A temporary table has the following special features:

A temporary table is created by using the CREATE TEMPORARY TABLE statement. Notice that the keyword TEMPORARY is added between the CREATE and TABLE keywords.

MySQL removes the temporary table automatically when the session ends, or the connection is terminated. Of course, you can use the DROP TABLE statement to remove a temporary table explicitly when you are no longer using it.

A temporary table is only available and accessible to the client that creates it. Different clients can create temporary tables with the same name. This will not cause any errors as only the client that creates the temporary table can see it

However, in the same session, two temporary tables cannot share the same name.

A temporary table can have the same name as a normal table in a database. For example, if you create a temporary table named person_info in the sample database, the existing person_info table becomes inaccessible. Every query you issue against the person_info table is now referring to the temporary table. When you drop the table temporary table, the permanent table is available and accessible.

Even though a temporary table can have the same name as a permanent table, it is not recommended. This may lead to confusion and potentially cause an unexpected loss of data.

For example, if the connection to the database server is lost and you reconnect to the server automatically, you cannot differentiate between the temporary table and the permanent one. Then, you may issue a DROP TABLE statement to remove the permanent table instead of the temporary table, which is not expected. To avoid this issue, you can use the DROP TEMPORARY TABLE statement to drop a temporary table.

The syntax of the CREATE TEMPORARY TABLE statement is like the syntax of the CREATE TABLE statement, except for the TEMPORARY keyword:

```
CREATE TEMPORARY TABLE table_name(
    column_1,
    column_2,
    ...
    column_n
);
```

To create a temporary table whose structure is based on an existing table, you cannot use the CREATE TEMPORARY TABLE LIKE statement. This can be accomplished by using the following syntax:

```
CREATE TEMPORARY TABLE temporary_table_name
```

```
SELECT * FROM original_table
LIMIT 0;
```

You can use the DROP TABLE statement to remove temporary tables; however, it is good practice to add the TEMPORARY keyword as follows:

```
DROP TEMPORARY TABLE table_name;
```

The DROP TEMPORARY TABLE statement removes a temporary table only, not a permanent table. It helps avoid the mistake of dropping a permanent table when you name your temporary table the same as the name of a permanent table.

For example, to remove the person_info temporary table, you use the following statement:

```
DROP TEMPORARY TABLE person_info;
```

Notice that if you try to remove a permanent table with the DROP TEMPORARY TABLE statement, you will get an error message saying that the table that you are trying to drop is unknown.

If you develop an application that uses a connection pooling or persistent connections, it is not guaranteed that the temporary tables are removed automatically when your application is terminated. Because the database connection that the application uses may still be open and placed in a connection pool for other clients to reuse later. Therefore, it is good practice to always remove the temporary tables whenever you no longer use them.

Chapter 9: Indexing and Performance

Indexing is especially important; it allow us to do the following:
1. Prevent queries from doing full scans of an entire dataset.
2. Access less and therefore lock fewer rows during queries.
3. Speed up queries drastically.
4. Prevent sorting records post fetching.
5. Impose constraints e.g. data uniqueness.
6. Join datasets efficiently.

All in all, good indexing can drastically improve response times.

Common problems when applying indexes are:
1. Having an index for every column in the table.
2. Not utilizing composite (multi-column) indexes.
3. Using composite indexes, but with ineffective column orderings that prevent the index being fully utilized.
4. Creating indexes based on rules of thumb or heuristics, such as indexing all columns that appear in the WHERE clause.

It is very important to be able to reason how indexes work and to choose them based on that understanding.

The purpose of an index is to allow you to retrieve data at a faster rate. Imagine you are trying to find your friends phone number. Now imagine that the only information you have is a large phone book consisting of first names, last names, and an associated phone number, which is stored in a completely random order.

Without the use of sorting, you would have to check every single entry in this phone book to find your friend. This is known as a table scan in the database world, an example of when a lookup uses no indexes. It is extremely inefficient, especially if it was a case where our phone book contained everyone in the world, billions of data records.

9.1 - Adding a single column index

On the off chance that we arranged this phonebook by last name. It would, at any rate, permit us to explore the indexes:

last_name	first_name	phone_number
Jones	Jenny	06481234500
Jones	John	06481234501
Jones	Bill	06481234502
Jones	Bush	06481234503
Jones	Andrew	06481234504
Jones	Steve	06481234505
Jones	Jim	06481234506
Jones	Shawn	06481234507

This is an example of a single column index on (last_name).

ALTER TABLE `phonebook` ADD INDEX (`last_name`);

In an enormous telephone directory, there can be many individuals with the exact same last name as your friend. For example, if there are 513 individuals with the last name Jones; however, there more than 4 million individuals with the last name 'Smith,' which means you can end up looking up over 4 million lines.

So, it's very clear that to find our friend effectively and efficiently, a one column index is not enough.

Why don't we put in an index on every column?
To do this, we can put in many columns like this:

ADD index last_name
ADD index first_name
ADD index phone_number

This can be envisioned as having three telephone directories, each arranged by the column you have placed an index on. This doesn't generally help you very much though. You can restructure this and use an Index Merge by crossing and combining the outcomes you find from every one of the three individual columns. However, this strategy is generally not very successful. Ordinarily, MySQL will just utilize one index, per table, per query, so things will be substantially more useful on the off chance that we plan to use a solitary index to fulfill our query.

9.2 - A Multiple Column Index

For this, we can start with last name, with the first name to follow.

ALTER TABLE `phonebook` ADD INDEX (`last_name`, `first_name`);

This is known as a merged index since we are indexing on a compound of different columns. In this example, a composite of (last_name, first_name). This index would sort sections as you would expect in an ordinary phonebook. Initially by last name, and afterward, by first name.

How the index has arranged sections would permit you to effectively find your friends' number, presumably following a method like what is highlighted in the table below:

last_name	first_name	phone_number
Jones	Joe	06481234400
Jones	Andrew	06481234401
Jones	**Ben**	06481234402
Jones	**Ben**	**06481234403**
Root	Alex	06481234404
Burns	Michael	06481234405
Broad	Archer	06481234406

By including a few columns in an index, we can rapidly limit the rows that have to be processed, which saves us from looking over a lot of unsorted columns as part of a table scan. The most significant thing to learn from this is how the result set has been sorted. The sorting of the data allows us to be proficient in narrowing down our search without having to perform any table scan. We can now effectively find our friend, Jones.

It is clear to see the order in which these columns are indexed, and thus how their sorting can limit how effective an index can be for a particular query.

As an example, the index we have just discussed (last_name, first_name) would not be beneficial for a query such as:

SELECT * FROM phonebook where first_name = 'James';

This is because we have not specified any criteria for the last_name. The index we built does not sort first names in any logical distribution that would allow us to quickly search through them, so instead, we must do a full table scan.

So far, we've discovered that:
- Utilizing composite indexes is crucial in the case where you are attempting to speed up a specific query.
- Index order is very important.

Examples:
INDEX (last, first)
WHERE last = … - *Good*
WHERE last = … AND first = … - *Good*
WHERE first = … AND last = … - *Good*
WHERE first = … - *Index Useless*
INDEX (a, b) VS INDEX (b, a)
WHERE a = 1 AND b = 3 - *Both work well*
WHERE b = 2 - *Second only*
WHERE a = 4 - *First only*
INDEX(a), INDEX(b) Is not the same as INDEX(a,b)
But using the two indexes (a),(b) can benefit from:
(SELECT … WHERE A …) UNION (SELECT … WHERE B …)

Since you get the essential idea of how sorting information in specific ways makes it a lot simpler to perform queries, it is time for us to discuss how indexing works in MySQL.

MySQL Architecture

MySQL allows us to utilize a wide array of different storage engines, these queries are parsed, optimized, and then MySQL, through a defined API, will interact with a chosen storage engine to retrieve and present data. Each storage engine has different properties that make it suitable for different use cases.

InnoDB Indexes

Most of our tables are set up by using the storage engine InnoDB, which utilizes B-Tree based indexes. We will discuss these exclusively (there are other types of indexes such as: hash indexes, full-text indexes, spatial R-tree indexes, all of which you can research if you want a more in-depth understanding of InnoDB indexes).

You can check what engines are being used for your tables by using the following MySQL query:

SHOW TABLE STATUS;
SELECT TABLE_NAME,ENGINE FROM information_schema.TABLES;

Like a binary search, B-trees allow effective lookups of key value pairs by sorting data into a data structure that can be traversed efficiently, avoiding the full scans we discussed earlier. You start from the root node and follow down towards the leaf nodes. Each node has a lower and an upper bound on keys that guide your search, pruning down the set of leaf nodes you are interested in.

When we add a new index, a B-Tree is constructed using the respective keys (dictated by which columns you've indexed).

When you issue a query to your database the MySQL optimizer will evaluate among all relevant indexes which you can use during lookups (the main cost metric is how much data the query will access).

An important thing to note is how Primary Key indexes and Secondary key indexes differ.

9.3 - Primary Key Indexes

Primary keys use a clustered index. It is considered clustered because the actual row data is stored, or clustered, together with the key.

In most cases, this will be a primary key that you have allocated yourself and there will be a unique identifier for every single row in your table.

In this case, the clustered index is literally the table itself, it is not a separate structure to the table.

Since the clustered index is the table in InnoDB, it is important to choose a suitable primary key, as this key will be used often. If you do not choose a logical primary key, you may have to restructure. Restructuring can be very expensive and can be very tricky and difficult to do.

Non-sequential primary keys can lead to fragmentation issues. This can cause page splits and disk fragmentations that can lead to overheads in input and output operations. Fragmentation is an unwanted problem where memory blocks cannot be allocated to the processes due to their small size and the blocks remain unused.

You should strive to insert data in primary key order when using InnoDB, and you should try to use a clustering key that will give monotonically increasing values for each new row. This will ensure that rows are inserted in sequential order and this will offer better performance for joins by using primary keys.

9.4 - Secondary Indexes

Obviously, there can only be one clustered index because you cannot store the row data in two places at once. Therefore, secondary indexes (any indexes we apply that are not the primary index) are not clustered, and are in fact, separate structures to the table itself.

The leaf nodes for secondary indexes do not store row data as the Primary Key B-Tree did, instead they simply store Primary Key values, which serve as pointers to the row data.

This means that when you are using a secondary index, InnoDB will first use the B-Tree of the secondary index to retrieve the Primary Key values of the applicable rows, and then after these values have been fetched, use these values in conjunction with the Primary Key B-tree to fetch the row data.

Since the Primary Key is appended to every secondary index in InnoDB, don't pick huge primary keys. Ideally keep them short so that it does not take too much memory. Remember that all data will be clustered into this primary key. Therefore, a bulky Primary Key will lead to bulky secondary indexes.

This additional lookup to follow the Primary Key 'pointer' from the secondary index has some overhead. It is still relatively quick because the primary key is indexed, but this is where the **covering index** optimization can come into effect.

9.5 - Covering Indexes

If your secondary index holds all the data needed to satisfy your query, it 'covers' it. If this is the case, you don't need to follow the Primary Key (PK) values to fetch any additional data.

If we go back to our first example of the phonebook, say we had an index on (`last_name`, `first_name`), and we ran a query such as:

SELECT phone_number FROM phonebook WHERE last_name = 'Jones' AND first_name = 'Michael'

We would be able to quickly retrieve the PK values for the records. However, to fetch the phone_number, we would still need to follow the PK values afterwards to fetch row data from the clustered Primary Key index. If we also added our phone_number column to our index, like so: (last_name, first_name, phone_number), the same query is now completely satisfied, or covered, by the index -- resulting in no additional lookups being required, making this query run much faster.

In general, an index is said to be covering if it can completely satisfy the data required by the query.

So far, indexes have shown to be useful in speeding up lookups on columns specified in the WHERE clause, and on data retrieval by covering columns specified in your projections.

9.6 - Indexes with ORDER and GROUP BY

Another overlooked factor is how indexes can be used in tandem with the ORDER and GROUPING BY operations.

Let's say you only have an index on (last_name) in your phone book, and you run the query:

SELECT * FROM phone_book WHERE last_name = 'Jones' ORDER BY first_name

This will use the last_name index as you would expect, to quickly narrow down the records with that last name. Unfortunately, you now need to perform a sort on these resulting records to get them sorted by first name. This is because the index did not sort the results by first_name in any meaningful way.

This is known as a File Sort, a sort that occurs after the query. It requires fetching the data into a temporary buffer and then sorting it before finally returning and displaying the data. This would not have been needed if the data were already sorted by the index.

This also applies even if you only wanted to read 5 rows. Say you ran the following:

SELECT last_name FROM phonebook WHERE first_name='Michael' ORDER BY last_name LIMIT 5.

You are still fetching thousands of records, sorting them, then only after this operation has completed: return the top 5 while discarding the rest of the records you spent time processing.

If we had indexed on both (`last_name`, `first_name`), we would not have needed to perform this extra sort because the records would have already been sorted for us in the order we wanted.

This is another important use case for indexes to avoid performing these file sorts. This also applies to GROUP BY statements. Imagine we executed the following query with this composite index on last_name and first_name:

SELECT * FROM phonebook WHERE last_name = 'Jones' GROUP BY first_name

The records would already be sorted by last_name, allowing us to quickly filter down the records with the last_name 'Jones.' After these results are returned, they are also sorted by first_name due to the second part of the index, meaning they are already grouped for us. We would not need to perform any additional sorting at the end, which would add further overheads to our query.

Indexes are useful not just for navigating tables quickly, but also for speeding up ORDER BY and GROUP BYs.

Ordering the results by the index only works when the order of the index is exactly the same as the ORDER BY clause and all columns are sorted in the same direction (ascending or descending).

INDEX (a,b)
- ORDER BY 'a' ASC, 'b' ASC - *Good*
- ORDER BY 'a' DESC, 'b' DESC - *Good*
- ORDER BY 'a' ASC, 'b' DESC - *Cannot use index*

The most efficient order to retrieve records is the one that the index sorts by. Any busy system should avoid ordering sets of records server-side, especially if paginating and reading subsets of ordered sets because they will access thousands of records each time.

9.7 - Effect of Indexes on JOIN

Indexes have a massive effect on the speed of JOIN operations. Let's say you have two tables: user, and user_meta_data (which has a column user_id that refers to the user table's PK id).

If both tables have 1000 records and you run the following query:

SELECT * FROM users JOIN user_meta_data ON user_meta_data.user_id = users.id;

For every row in the users table, MySQL will perform a lookup in the user_meta_data table to join on the id onto user_id.

Without any indexes on user_meta_data (specifically without an index on user_id) MySQL would have to perform a table scan, looking at all 1000 rows for each lookup. This would require over (1000*1000) or 1 million comparisons, so it is going to be very slow.

By adding an index on the user_meta_data, as well as on the user_id column, we can prevent these 1000 comparisons per row, allowing the indexes B-tree to be used for each join lookup.

Deferred Join Optimization

Imagine a case where you have an index on (gender, rating) and you are trying to run the following query:

SELECT gender, rating, age, height, <cols> FROM profiles WHERE gender='M' ORDER BY rating LIMIT 100000, 10;

This query is skipping the first 100,000 rows (the offset), before returning just 10.

This will work as you might expect, it will use the index to scan over all of the 100,000 records (no it isn't smart enough to simply hop to the offset) and because the index is not covering, it will be pulling the additional column data, such as age and height by using the Primary Key B-Tree as we mentioned earlier. After pointlessly pulling all this data: 100,000 of the 100,010 records are thrown away because we only wanted 10. Clearly pulling the extra data for the 100,000 was unnecessary work.

A good strategy for optimizing such queries is to use a deferred join instead, which is a term for using a covering index to retrieve only the primary key columns of the rows that you will eventually need. This avoids pulling in the extra columns that cause wasted overheads.

After you have retrieved these primary keys, you can simply perform a join back onto the original table to retrieve all desired columns. This helps minimize the amount of work MySQL must do in gathering data that it will only be thrown away later.

Going back to our example:

SELECT gender, rating, age, height, <cols> FROM profiles INNER JOIN (SELECT <primary key cols> FROM profiles WHERE x.gender='M' ORDER BY rating LIMIT 100000, 10) AS x USING(<primary key cols>);

The sub query only accesses the primary key columns, thus no additional overheads occur when data, which is not included in the index, is pulled. This is a covering index and is going to be noticeably quicker. After we have the 10 primary key values that we are interested in, we perform a join on these results, fetching the extra columns we wanted in the first place. In this case, we only suffer the overhead of fetching the extra columns for 10 records, which is a lot quicker than doing it for all 100,000.

This is especially useful if the column you are wanting to select is very large, with a data type of TEXT or BLOB because the overhead will be much more substantial.

Usually the less records you are trying to access, the less overheads you will experience, and the faster your response times will be.

So how can you check if your indexes are being used? This is usually easy, simply use the EXPLAIN statement.

9.8 - THE EXPLAIN Statement

The explain statement, is very useful for explaining how your query is executing, and therefore revealing why it could be slow. When you put EXPLAIN in front of your query, you will be provided with information from the MySQL optimizer about the statement execution plan. This information can include:

- The indexes it is considering using.
- The order in which it plans to join tables.
- The indexes it actually used.
- How many rows will be accessed?
- Whether it used a filesort.

EXPLAIN works with SELECT, DELETE, INSERT, REPLACE, and UPDATE statements.

You should use the data from the explain statement to drive your investigation. It can indicate which indexes are missing or not being used, as well as many other inefficiencies in your query or schema. The information shown can appear as follows:

```
id: 1
select_type: SIMPLE
table: categories
type: ALL
possible_keys: NULL
key: NULL
key_len: NULL
ref: NULL
rows: 4
Extra:
1 row in set (0.00 sec)
```

I won't go into detail about each of these columns, however there are a few key ones to look at when evaluating your indexes. These are:

- *Possible keys* – shows the keys that can be used by MySQL to find rows from the table. If this is NULL, it indicates that no useful indexes can be applied.
- *Key* – indicates the actual index that MySQL used.
- *Rows* – shows the number of records that were examined to produce the output. This is especially relevant during JOINs.
- *Key_len* – longest length of the key that was used, i.e. which parts of the composite index are being used. Use this to figure out how many columns were used from it.
- *Ref* – which columns, or constants are compared to the index to select rows.

The other column that is worth mentioning is the Extra column, which contains additional info:

- *Using index* — MySQL was able to use a covering index.
- *Distinct* — MySQL stops searching after it found the first matching row.

What you don't want to see in Extra:

- *Using file sort* — this means that extra sorting was required.
- *Using temporary* — a temp table was needed.
- *Using join buffer* — tables processed in large batches of rows, instead of using index lookups.
- *Using where* — after fetching rows from storage engine, extra filtering needed to happen for each row. This can be acceptable if only a few rows were returned.

It should be clear by now that Indexes need to be designed for the whole query, not just for the WHERE clause.

More on Index Order
In a B-Tree the index is sorted first by the leftmost column, then by the next column, and so on, as we have already seen. This greatly affects how useful an index will be and it is one of the most important things to get correct.

How to pick a logical order?
This relies upon the query that will make use of the index — you must pick an index that permits:

- Your WHERE conditionals to effectively look-up data.
- Your rows to be sorted and grouped in a way beneficial to the query.
- Your Joins to be efficient.

Index Selectivity
Index selectivity is the ratio of the number of distinct indexed values (the cardinality) to the total number of rows in the table (#T).

It ranges from 1/#T to 1. A unique index has a selectivity of 1, which is as good as it gets.

Using the phonebook example: an index of (first_name, last_name) might be less effective than (last_name, first_name) because first names are much less distinct when compared to last_names, meaning it can narrow down less results.

Therefore, if order is not important between two columns, choose the most selective (narrows down to less records) first.

Range Queries

Similar to what we have just explained with the prefix rule, the moment you use a range query on a column in your index, you have gone as far as you can utilizing this index.

If you issued a range query such as:

SELECT * FROM phonebook WHERE last_name LIKE 'J%' AND first_name ='Michael';ADD INDEX (last_name, first_name, phone_number)

This would utilize the first part (last_name) of our index, allowing us to quickly satisfy the range conditional and find all of the rows with the last_name beginning with 'J.' However after this, there is no way our B-Tree can be further utilized to quickly filter on first_name.

If you are utilizing an index for range queries, try to ensure the column you are performing the range over is ordered last within the index. Similarly, you cannot use an index to perform range queries on two columns for the points already mentioned.

Index Condition Pushdown

That being said, there is a technique called Index Condition Pushdown that can help us with the issue outlined above.

Index pushdowns essentially allow us to push index conditions down to the database engine so that MySQL does not have to return irrelevant rows that would only be filtered out later.

This means that in some cases we can still use an index past a range condition. It would be best to experiment and test to see the results for yourself. Regardless of the situation, MySQL will be at its most effective if you are able to leave range columns towards the end of your index. Index Condition Pushdowns should only be used when you cannot find a viable alternative.

Typically, we can only use the leftmost prefix of the index.

- You may need to have indexes on the same columns in different orders depending on your queries.
- Try to use as many columns as possible up to the first range of the query – after a range, no other index column can be used. So put the index that is likely to be ranged right at the end.

Prefix Ranges

SELECT ... WHERE last_name LIKE '%ones'

This is not a range; we can't use a B-Tree to traverse this. Imagine yourself being at the root of a tree with such a query, do you go left or right? You don't know! This is exactly why we can use an index to support such a query.

Examples:

INDEX (a, b) VS INDEX (b, a)

WHERE a = 1 AND b > 3 – *First is better*

WHERE b = 5 AND b > 7 – *Second is better*

WHERE a > 1 AND b > 3 – *Each stops after 1st Column*

WHERE b = 2 – *Second only*

WHERE b > 2 – *Second only*

WHERE a = 4 – *First only*

WHERE a > 4 – *First only*

INDEX (a, b, c)

WHERE a > 1 AND b =3 AND c = 4 – *Uses only first part of index*

WHERE a = 1 AND b > 3 AND c = 4 – *Uses first 2 parts of index*

WHERE a = 1 AND b = 3 AND c = 4 — *Uses all of index*

SKIP SCAN

Let's say you have got a table of users with columns: gender, last_name, first_name, age, etc.

If you had an index on (gender, last_name, first_name) and you wanted to run the query:

SELECT first_name, last_name, WHERE last_name = 'Jones' AND first_name = 'Michael'.

As you know, your index will not facilitate this. Imagine being at the root of a tree, you can either traverse left for male and continue using the index, or instead go to the right for female, but you cannot go in both directions at once. However, if you rewrite our query to instead use our index as:

SELECT first_name, last_name, WHERE gender IN('male','female') AND last_name = 'Jones' AND first_name = 'Michael';

You can think of this as allowing MySQL to enumerate each value (in this case 'gender') separately, allowing us to dive into the rest of the index from there. Upon finishing the enumeration of each value, we can simply UNION the results.
In this case, we use 'M' as the gender, so we can utilize the whole of the remaining index for the query. After this, we would use 'F' as our starting point, and again we would be able to utilize our whole index to satisfy the query. Finally, we can simply union the resulting sets of 'M' & 'F' to get all the rows we're interested in.

This works well when the column being used in the IN has a relatively small range of values. However, its efficiency may vary. If you have any doubts, measure the response times of your index changes, and add new indexes if you see that they are needed. Don't force yourself into using a single index that attempts to satisfy everything for the sake of it!

Ambiguous Queries

Ambiguous queries will be slow because MySQL cannot utilize indexes to prevent table scans:

INDEX ON phonebook (town, first_name, last_name)

SELECT * FROM phonebook WHERE town <> 'MPK' and first_name = 'Michael'

SELECT * FROM phonebook WHERE town NOT IN ('MPK', 'SEA') and first_name = 'Michael'

MySQL won't be able to use the index for these queries, However the optimizer can easily work with this instead:

SELECT * FROM phonebook WHERE town IN('KY', 'SEA', 'NYC') and first_name = 'Michael'

In general, all the below could leave an index unusable:

- *!=*
- *<>*
- *NOT LIKE, NOT IN...*
- *NOT EXISTS (SELECT * ...) — essentially a LEFT JOIN, often efficient*
- *NOT (expression)*

Don't use functions on columns in your queries

MySQL generally cannot use indexes on columns unless the columns are isolated in the query. So do not use functions or expressions on columns in your queries.

The expression on the left should be a column e.g. <column> <operator> <value>

The moment you use: func(column) <operator> <value> you can no longer use the index and a full table scan will occur.

Examples:
- WHERE id+3 = 4; *— Bad*

- WHERE start_date + INTERVAL 1 YEAR > NOW() – *Bad*
- WHERE YEAR(start_date) = 2015 AND MONTH(start_date) = 1 – *Bad*
- Where number +0 = 5; – *Bad*
- WHERE func(number) = n; – *Bad*
- WHERE number = 5+4; – *Good*
- WHERE number = func(n); – *Good*
- WHERE start_date > NOW() — INTERVAL 1 YEAR – *Good*
- WHERE start_date BETWEEN '2015–01–01' AND '2015–01–31' – Good

9.9 - Redundant indexes

Over indexing can hurt performance due to the unnecessary overhead that may occur. The major disadvantage of having too many indexes is the maintenance cost.

Adding new indexes might have a performance impact for INSERT, UPDATE, and DELETE operations, especially if a new index causes you to hit memory limits.

Every time you perform a write on a table, the indexes will need to be maintained. Furthermore, when you run a query, each index must be considered by the MySQL Optimizer.

- If there is an index on (A, B), adding another index (A) would be redundant because it is a prefix of the first index. That is, the index on (A, B) can already be used as an index for column A alone.
- If there is an index on (A, PK_ID). The PK_ID column as you already know is already included if you are using InnoDB, so it is redundant, luckily it won't add it twice, so you are safe to do it – you just don't need to.

You can easily see which indexes are redundant, especially those that have never been used, by querying the INFORMATION_SCHEMA database.

That being said do not hesitate to add indexes that will be frequently used. In a read heavy application, the costs will be negligible.

9.10 - Index Merge

When I said that MySQL only uses one index per query per table, most of the time this is true. However, there are some occasions where MySQL does have the capabilities to use multiple single column indexes.

For example, it can use several indexes to fetch primary key values, and then perform a union or intersection depending on the query. These are useful in situations where you cannot form a suitable multicolumn index like in the case of several 'OR' conditional operators in your query.

However, it is rare that these are used, and if you are able to form a suitable multicolumn index, then you should. This will typically outperform a merge index.

9.11 - Constraint Indexes

Do not enforce uniqueness at an application level. Use unique indexes when you need something to be unique. Attempting to do this with application code is always going to cause issues further down the line. Some of these issues may be the following:

- Hidden code paths bypassing validations, especially with FBcode, WWW etc. developers need to be aware of to run these checks before mutating the database.
- People manipulating the DB directly.
- Application code running in parallel to different transactions may have inconsistent views of the database, thus making enforcing constraints very difficult.

Soft Deletes

Soft delete, setting a deleted flag instead of deleting, is a great way to ensure the ability to recover accidentally deleted data by users for many applications. If you need to support soft deletes, you can achieve this by implementing one of the following methods:

- Prefixing a NULLABLE 'active' tinyint(1) (default 1) column to your unique index.
- Adding a 'deleted_time stamp' (default 0) within the unique index.

- Adding a UUID deletion token (default some constant) within the unique index.
- Create a separate 'deleted_' table and move records there when they are deleted.

Which method is the best?

- The advantage of the 'active' column is that it's quite simple to configure. Due to the way InnoDB works, it won't treat NULLS as duplicates, which is exactly why this method works. Non deleted records will have a value like '1' that prevent duplicates. Deleted records however will have a value of NULL allowing several 'deleted' duplicates.
- The advantage of the delete_time_stamp / UUID token method is that they do not need to be prefixes, we can put them at the end of the index ordering. This can provide better performance when searching, because our index columns will be initially more selective than the 'active' column, allowing potentially faster inserts (each time we try and insert, this index will need to be traversed to check for a duplicate).
- The downside to the UUID token is having to generate it, and due to its random distribution, it can cause fragmentation overheads later; furthermore, its size may cause overheads.
- The deleted_time_stamp provides good performance with little effort.
- Creating a separate table provides great 'read' performance: reducing table sizes, allowing you to use a normal unique index, and allowing everyday searches to scan less records. The downside being you must move these records between tables.
- My recommendation is to use the deleted_time_stamp approach and then if you find a performance need later, you can move to using a separate 'deleted_table.'

9.12 - What columns should I Index?

This is dependent on a lot of different factors, such as:

- What columns you're going to query.
- What JOINs you'll perform.
- What ORDER/GROUP BYs, etc.

- Find your slow queries (from slow query log) if you do not have any in mind and see what indexes might speed them up. Use EXPLAIN to see what indexes are currently in use and apply better indexing. Use EXPLAIN again to ensure your new index was effective.
- Unsure about which column order? Then use the most selective, unless you need a range or order.
- Don't index a column with low selectivity e.g. 'gender' on its own. If WHERE gender = 'M' occurs >20% of results, the index might not be that effective (the optimizer may favor a table scan instead). In these cases, simply run tests on response times to guide your decisions.
- Query the INFORMATION SCHEMA database to see stats on your indexes and tables, these can really help guide performance tuning.
- Use the unused index script linked earlier to find index failures.
- Index design is not separate from table design. They go hand in hand, and you must design everything to suit your queries.

9.13 - Star system

A good way to measure the quality of an index is by using the star system, with the goal being to achieve all three stars:

1. The index earns one star if it places relevant rows adjacent to each other, or at least as close to each other as possible. This minimizes the thickness of the index slice that must be scanned. The goal is to narrow down the number of rows that need to be scanned as much as possible. To gain this star, you can pick the columns from all equal predicates in the WHERE clause. Many people think the purpose of an index is to find individual rows, but finding single rows leads to random disk operations (which is slow). It is much more efficient to find groups of rows, all, or most of which are interesting, rather than to find them one at a time. Therefore, a good index will group keys together in such a way that this is achieved effectively.

2. A second star is earned if the index sorts the rows in the order the query needs, avoiding additional file sorts.

3. A final star is earned if the index covers all the columns needed for the query, i.e., it is a covering index. All the columns in the SELECT appear in the index.

Of course, depending on your query, it might not be possible to achieve all three.

9.14 - Other considerations

When the number of rows you have in your database table reaches the millions, you must think deeply about data types and indexes. A lightweight data type can save a lot of overhead for a large table, especially if it allows more of that table to be stored in memory.

When rows get into billions, summary tables (e.g. storing counts) can be very effective.

Deleted flags with low cardinality may perform badly or just not be used at all. A potential workaround can be to move deleted rows into another table.

If you need to index on a large string column, consider only indexing on a prefix or hash of that column, which will help avoid overly large indexes.

9.15 - How will MySQL choose an index?

The MySQL optimizer evaluates between a set of indexes for each query to determine which one will be most useful based on a cost metric, this typically being how much data the query will access.

For single table queries, the set of indexes that are evaluated can be any index including columns appearing in the WHERE clause. For JOINs on multiple tables, the MySQL optimizer will try to figure out which table can be narrowed down the most by the passed in predicates (just like in the single table query), and then it will calculate how many rows the whole join would have to scan based on the table statistics (table size/indexes). When obvious query plans do not exist, a change in these statistics may result in ambiguous plan choices.

You can see the indexes your query considers by using EXPLAIN as mentioned earlier.

9.16 - Testing an index

When testing out your indexes make sure you have copied a reasonable sample of production data to run tests on. Testing on fake data with different distributions to production data will not reflect production performance.

Test your index with all the reasonable arguments, different query conditions can use very different indexes.

Be aware that there are various cases where the engine may do something better than expected.

Sometimes you may not be able to find a perfect index for your query, in which case you can consider rewriting your query.

Chapter 10: Data Altering Commands

There are times when we wish to change the data that already exists within our database. We can achieve this by making use of data alerting commands. We will be covering UPDATE and DELETE commands.

10.1 - Using UPDATE

One of the most useful commands in SQL is the UPDATE command. This allows us to update existing values in our database. This saves us from performing the more arduous task of deleting records and adding them back with the new values. There may be a requirement where the existing data in a MySQL table needs to be modified. You can do so by using the SQL UPDATE command. This will modify any field value of any MySQL table.

The syntax for the UPDATE command is as follows.

UPDATE table_name
SET column_1 = new_value_1, column_2 = new_value_2
[WHERE Clause] -- *Optional, but necessary in many cases*

You can update one or more column at a time, specify any condition using the WHERE clause, and update the values in a single table at a time. The WHERE clause is very useful when you want to update the selected rows in a table.

Let's apply this information to a practical example:

```
UPDATE person_info
SET LastName = 'Rogers'
WHERE PersonID in (2, 3);
```

What if we wanted to update the last name of some people in our person_info table? This can be easily performed by using the UPDATE command. Look at the SQL query above.

UPDATE person_info, this is specifying that we want to update data values in the person_info table.

SET LastName = 'Rogers,' this is what we want the new value of the LastName column to be.

Where PersonID in (2,3), this is probably the most important section. This part of the query states that we **only want to update the values where the PersonID is equal to 2 or 3**. This is especially important. If we did not include this statement it would have updated all our LastName values to 'Rogers.'

10.2 - Using DELETE

There are some cases where we want to completely remove data from database. For this, we use the DELETE command. Be careful when using this command, as once you have deleted a record from your database, it is gone forever! There will also be no warning messages or prompts from MySQL asking you 'Are you sure you would like to delete this record?' This means you must be incredibly careful if you plan on using this command.

The syntax for using DELETE is as follows:

DELETE FROM table_name [WHERE Clause]

If the WHERE clause is not specified, then all the records will be deleted from the given MySQL table.

You can specify any condition using the WHERE clause. You can delete records in a single table at a time. The WHERE clause is very useful when you want to delete selected rows in a table.

Let's apply this to a practical example:

```
DELETE FROM city_info
WHERE CityID = 7
```

We have our city_info table already in existence containing information about various cities. What if we no longer need to track the information for one of these cities and want to delete the record from our database? We simply find the unique CityID for this city and insert the value into the WHERE clause of our DELETE FROM command.

DELETE FROM city_info, we specify what table we wish to delete from.
WHERE CityID = 7, this states the exact record we want to delete from our table.

When trying to update records in MySQL workbench, you may encounter 'Error Code: 1175 You are using safe update mode and you tried to update a table without a WHERE that uses a KEY column.'

This occurs because your MySQL session has the safe-updates option set. This means that you cannot update or delete records without specifying a key in the WHERE clause. To avoid this, execute the following query:

This will prevent this error from occurring when using your UPDATE statements.

> Give It A Try! Try out the UPDATE and DELETE commands. Use UPDATE to make PersonIDs 1, 2, and 3 have the same last name. Also, DELETE one of the cities in the city_info table that does not have a person from that city.

10.3 - Using TRUNCATE

TRUNCATE is an alternate method of deleting records from the table. The MySQL TRUNCATE TABLE statement allows you to delete all data in a table. Logically, the TRUNCATE TABLE statement is like a DELETE statement without a WHERE clause that deletes all rows from a table. It also performs the same functionality as using the DROP TABLE statement followed by a CREATE TABLE statement. However, the

TRUNCATE TABLE statement is more efficient than the DELETE statement because it drops and recreates the table instead of deleting rows one by one.

Here is the basic syntax of the TRUNCATE TABLE statement:

TRUNCATE [TABLE] table_name;

table_name - the name of the table which you want to remove all data for.

TABLE - This keyword is optional. However, it is good practice to use the TABLE keyword to distinguish between the TRUNCATE TABLE statement and the TRUNCATE() function.

If there are any FOREIGN KEY constraints from other tables, which reference the table that you truncate, the TRUNCATE TABLE statement will fail. A truncate operation causes an implicit commit; therefore, it cannot be rolled back. The TRUNCATE TABLE statement also resets the current value in the AUTO_INCREMENT field. The TRUNCATE TABLE statement does not fire any DELETE triggers that may be associated with the table that is being truncated. Unlike a DELETE statement, the number of rows affected by the TRUNCATE TABLE statement is 0, which should be interpreted as no information.

Let's look at a practical example of using the TRUNCATE TABLE statement.

TRUNCATE TABLE person_info;

10.4 - DELETE vs. TRUNCATE

Although DELETE and TRUNCATE TABLE seem to have the same effect, they work differently. Here are some major differences between these two statements:

1. DELETE allows you to filter which rows are to be deleted based upon an optional WHERE clause, whereas TRUNCATE TABLE doesn't support the WHERE clause, it just removes all the rows.
2. TRUNCATE TABLE is faster and uses fewer system resources than DELETE, because DELETE scans the table to generate a count of rows that were affected, then delete the rows one by one, and record an entry in the

database log for each deleted row, while TRUNCATE TABLE just deletes all the rows without providing any additional information.

3. TRUNCATE TABLE statements drop and re-create the table in such a way that any auto-increment value is reset to its start value, which is generally 1.

Use TRUNCATE TABLE if you just want to delete all the rows and re-create the whole table. Use DELETE if you want to delete limited number of rows based on specific condition or you do not want to reset the auto-increment value.

10.5 - CAST

The MySQL CAST function converts a value from one datatype to another datatype.

The syntax for the CAST function in MySQL is as follows:

CAST(value AS type)
value – The value to convert to another datatype.
type – The datatype that you wish to convert value to.

It can be one of the following:

Value	Description
DATE	Converts value to DATE type, which has a date portion only. Format is 'YYYY-MM-DD.' Supported range is '1000-01-01' to '9999-12-31.'
DATETIME	Converts value to DATETIME type, which has both date and time portions. Format is 'YYYY-MM-DD HH:MM:SS.' Supported range is '1000-01-01 00:00:00' to '9999-12-31 23:59:59.'
TIME	Converts value to TIME type, which has a time portion only. Format is 'HH:MM:SS'. Supported range is '-838:59:59' to '838:59:59.'
CHAR	Converts value to CHAR type, which is a fixed length string.

SIGNED	Converts value to SIGNED type, which is a signed 64-bit integer.
UNSIGNED	Converts value to UNSIGNED type, which is an unsigned 64-bit integer.
BINARY	Converts value to BINARY type, which is a binary string.

Let's look at some practical examples of how we can use the CAST function.

SELECT CAST('2020-02-28' AS DATE);
Result: '2020-02-28'
This CAST example takes the value '2020-02-28' and casts it as a DATE data type.

SELECT CAST('2020-02-28 08:14:57' AS DATETIME);
Result: '2020-02-28 08:14:57'
This CAST example takes the value '2020-02-28 08:14:57' and casts it as a DATETIME data type.

SELECT CAST('08:14:57' AS TIME);
Result: '08:14:57'
This CAST example takes the value '08:14:57' and casts it as a TIME data type.

SELECT CAST(125 AS CHAR);
Result: '125'
This CAST example takes the value 125 and casts it as a CHAR data type with the value of '125.'

SELECT CAST(3-4 AS SIGNED);
Result: -1
This CAST example takes the value 3-4 and casts it as a SIGNED datatype with the value of -1.

SELECT CAST(4-6 AS UNSIGNED);
Result: 18446744073709551614
This CAST example takes the value 4-6 and casts it as an UNSIGNED datatype with the value of 18446744073709551614.

SELECT CAST('4' AS BINARY);

Result: '4'

This CAST example takes the value '4' and casts it as a BINARY datatype with the binary string value of '4.'

10.6 - CONVERT

The MySQL CONVERT function converts a value from one data type to another, or one-character set to another.

There are two valid forms of syntax for the CONVERT function, one syntax to convert data types and one syntax to convert character sets.

The first syntax for the CONVERT function is used to convert one data type to another data type in MySQL:

CONVERT(value, type)

OR

CONVERT(value USING character_set)

value – The value to convert.
character_set – The character set to convert to.
type – The data type that you wish to convert value to. Type can be one of the following:

Value	Description
DATE	Converts value to DATE type, which has a date portion only. Format is 'YYYY-MM-DD.' Supported range is '1000-01-01' to '9999-12-31.'
DATETIME	Converts value to DATETIME type, which has both date and time portions. Format is 'YYYY-MM-DD HH:MM:SS.' Supported range is '1000-01-01 00:00:00' to '9999-12-31 23:59:59.'
TIME	Converts value to TIME type, which has a time portion only.

	Format is 'HH:MM:SS.' Supported range is '-838:59:59' to '838:59:59.'
CHAR	Converts value to CHAR type, which is a fixed length string.
SIGNED	Converts value to SIGNED type, which is a signed 64-bit integer.
UNSIGNED	Converts value to UNSIGNED type, which is an unsigned 64-bit integer.
BINARY	Converts value to BINARY type, which is a binary string.

Let's look at practical examples for the CONVERT function.

SELECT CONVERT('2020-02-28', DATE);
Result: '2020-02-28'
This CONVERT example takes the value '2020-02-28' and converts it to a DATE data type.

SELECT CONVERT('2020-02-28 08:14:57', DATETIME);
Result: '2020-02-28 08:14:57'
This CONVERT example takes the value '2020-02-28 08:14:57' and converts it to a DATETIME data type.

SELECT CONVERT('08:14:57', TIME);
Result: '08:14:57'
This CONVERT example takes the value '08:14:57' and converts it to a TIME data type.

SELECT CONVERT(125, CHAR);
Result: '125'
This CONVERT example takes the value 125 and converts it as a CHAR data type with the value of '125.'

SELECT CONVERT(4-6, SIGNED);
Result: -2
This CONVERT example takes the value 4-6 and converts it as a SIGNED data type with the value of -2.

Convert to UNSIGNED

This CONVERT function example shows how to convert a value to an UNSIGNED type. For example:

SELECT CONVERT(4-6, UNSIGNED);
Result: 18446744073709551614
This CONVERT example takes the value 4-6 and converts it as an UNSIGNED datatype with the value of 18446744073709551614.

SELECT CONVERT('4', BINARY);
Result: '4'
This CONVERT example takes the value '4' and converts it as a BINARY datatype with the binary string value of '4.'

The second syntax for the MySQL CONVERT function allows you to convert a value from one-character set to another. Let's look at how to use the CONVERT function to convert between character sets. For example:

mysql> SELECT CONVERT('HelloThere' USING utf8);
Result: 'HelloThere'
This CONVERT example takes the value 'HelloThere' and converts it from the current character set to the utf8 character set.

We can change our example above to convert the value 'HelloThere' to the latin1 character set as follows:

SELECT CONVERT('HelloThere' USING latin1);
Result: 'HelloThere'

10.7 - CAST vs. CONVERT

Data conversion is one of the most frequent activities in a database. This is the reason why there are two available functions for this particular action.

Both CAST and CONVERT are functions used to convert one data type to another data type. They are mainly used in the MySQL program, and both are often used interchangeably. MySQL provides both functions to enable a user to change a data type and convert it to another if needed. Both CAST and CONVERT provide a way to write program procedures or queries. In many instances, both CAST and CONVERT are used in combination and with each other to achieve certain effects in the data. Without using CAST or CONVERT functions, implicit conversions occur.

The first difference between CAST and CONVERT is that CAST is an ANSI standard, while CONVERT is a specific function in the SQL server. There are also differences when it comes to what a particular function can and cannot do.

For example, a CONVERT function can be used for formatting purposes especially for date/time, data type, and money/data type. Meanwhile, CAST is used to remove or reduce format while still converting. Also, CONVERT can stimulate set date format options while CAST cannot do this function.

CAST is also the more portable function of the two. This means that the CAST function can be used by many databases. CAST is also less powerful and less flexible than CONVERT. On the other hand, CONVERT allows more flexibility and is the preferred function to use for data, time values, traditional numbers, and money signifiers. CONVERT is also useful in formatting the data's format.

CAST functions restore the decimals and numerical values to integers while converting. It also can be used to truncate the decimal portion or value of an integer.

There are also differences in the CAST and CONVERT syntax. The syntax of CAST is very simple. It includes the value to convert and the type of resulting data type. It has 'AS' as keywords to separate the data type from the value. There is an option to express the length, which is the integer that specifies the length of the target data type.

On the other hand, the CONVERT syntax mentions the resulting data type first along with the optional length. There is another expression and another optional parameter called style in the CONVERT function. Style allows formatting the data type and specifies how the CONVERT function should translate or format the data type. The CONVERT function doesn't need a keyword to separate the values and the data type.

Summary:
1. CAST and CONVERT are two SQL functions used by programmers to convert one data type to another.

2. The CAST function is ANSI standard and is compatible to use in other databases, while the CONVERT function is a specific function of the SQL server.

3. Since the CAST function is compatible with other databases, it is also described as portable, though it has fewer features compared to the CONVERT function. The CONVERT function, meanwhile, can do some things that the CAST function cannot.

4. The CAST function is used to convert a data type without a specific format. The CONVERT function does the converting and formatting of data types at the same time.

5. In terms of syntax, both functions have the optional parameter of length. In the CONVERT function, there is an additional parameter called style, which specifies the format of the data type after conversion.

6. The CAST function is often used to preserve decimal values and places, while converting them into integers. The function can also truncate the decimal value if needed. The CONVERT function cannot perform this task.

Chapter 11: The GROUP BY Clause and Aggregate Functions

The MySQL GROUP BY clause is used to group rows into subgroups based on values of columns or expressions. The GROUP BY clause groups a set of rows into a set of summary rows by values of columns or expressions. The GROUP BY clause returns one row for each group. In other words, it reduces the number of rows in the result set.

You often use the GROUP BY clause with aggregate functions such as SUM, AVG, MAX, MIN, and COUNT. The aggregate function that appears in the SELECT clause provides information about each group. An aggregate function performs a calculation on multiple values and returns a single value. For example, you can use the AVG() aggregate function that takes multiple numbers and returns the average value of the numbers.

The GROUP BY clause is an optional clause of the SELECT statement.
The GROUP BY clause has the following syntax:

```
SELECT column_1, column_2... column_n, aggregate_function(column_x)
FROM table_name
WHERE where_conditions
GROUP BY column_1, column_2... column_n;
```

The GROUP BY clause must appear after the FROM and WHERE clauses. Following the GROUP BY keywords is a list of comma-separated columns or expressions that you want to use as criteria to group the rows.

MySQL evaluates the GROUP BY clause after the FROM, WHERE, and SELECT clauses and before the HAVING, ORDER BY, and LIMIT clauses:

Let's apply the GROUP BY clause to a practical example.

We are going to break down the following SQL query:

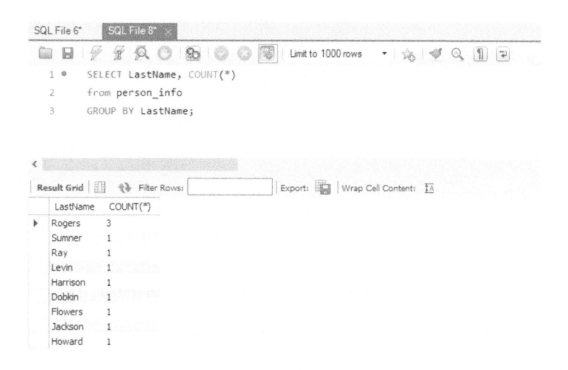

SELECT LastName, COUNT(*), we want to show the last names of the people in our table. We also want to get the count of each of the last names as they occur in our table.

From person_info, this is the table containing our data.

GROUP BY LastName, groups our records and allows our Results Grid to show:

LastName   COUNT(*)
Rogers   3

Without GROUP BY LastName the COUNT(*) aggregate function would not work as expected.

11.1 - Aggregate Functions

The COUNT function is an aggregate function that returns the number of rows in a table. The COUNT function allows you to count all rows or only rows that match a specified condition.

The COUNT function has three forms: COUNT(*), COUNT(expression), and COUNT(DISTINCT expression):

1. COUNT(*) function
   The COUNT(*) function returns the number of rows in a
   result set returned by a SELECT statement. The COUNT(*) returns the
   number of rows including duplicate, non-NULL, and NULL rows.

2. COUNT(expression)
   The COUNT(expression) returns the number of rows that do not contain
   NULL values as the result of the expression.

3. COUNT(DISTINCT expression)
   The COUNT(DISTINCT expression) returns the number of distinct rows that
   do not contain NULL values as the result of the expression.

The return type of the COUNT() function is BIGINT. The COUNT() function returns
0 if there is no matching row found.

The COUNT(*) function is often used with a GROUP BY clause to return the
number of elements in each group.

Let's apply this information to a practical example by breaking down the following
SQL query to get a better understanding of how the COUNT function works:

```
1 •   SELECT COUNT(*) FROM person_info as pi
2     INNER JOIN city_info as ci ON ci.City = pi.City AND ci.State = pi.State
3
```

Result Grid | Filter Rows: | Export: | Wrap Cell Content: ‡A

COUNT(*)
9

SELECT COUNT(*) FROM person_info as pi. Here we are specifying that we want to count all the rows returned from the table person_info. Note the alias 'pi' we are using to represent this table.

INNER JOIN city_info as ci ON ci.City = pi.City AND ci.State = pi.State, this states that we want to retrieve the records from city_info also, but only where the City and State columns match for each table.

11.2 - MIN() and MAX()

The MAX function returns the maximum value in a set of values. The MAX function is useful in many cases, such as finding the greatest number, the most expensive product, and the largest payment from customers, and other such examples.

Here is the basic syntax of the MAX() function :

MAX(expression)

An example of the MAX function might look as follows:

SELECT MAX(PersonID)
FROM person_info;

In this example, the MAX function checks all values in the PersonID column of the person_info table to find the highest value.

The MIN function returns the minimum value in a set of values. The MIN function acts as an opposite action to the MAX function, and as such, can be applied to similar scenarios such as finding the smallest number, selecting the least expensive product, or getting the lowest credit limit.

Here is the basic syntax of the MIN function:

MIN(expression);

In this syntax, the MIN function accepts an expression, which can be a column or a valid expression that involves columns.

The DISTINCT has no effect on the MIN() function like other aggregate functions such as SUM(), AVG()and COUNT().

An example of the MAX function might look as follows:

SELECT MIN(PersonID)
FROM person_info;

In this example, the MIN function checks all values in the PersonID column of the person_info table to find the lowest value.

Whenever we select a column alongside MAX or MIN, make sure that the column is a part of GROUP BY clause.

MAX() or MIN() can also be applied on VARCHAR data type, in which case it will return the first or last value in alphabetical order.

11.3 - AVG()

The MySQL AVG function or 'average' function is an aggregate function that allows you to calculate the average value of a set. The average of a set of values is the number expressing the central or typical value in a dataset, in particular the mean, which is calculated by dividing the sum of the values in the set by their number.

This is the syntax for using the AVG function:

AVG([DISTINCT] expression)
Note the [DISTINCT] is optional.

You use the DISTINCT operator in the AVG function to calculate the average value of the distinct values. For example, if you have a set of values such as: 8, 8, 9, and 10, the AVG function with the DISTINCT operator will return 9 (8 + 9 + 10 / 3).

Let's apply this information to a practical example. Examine the SQL command below:

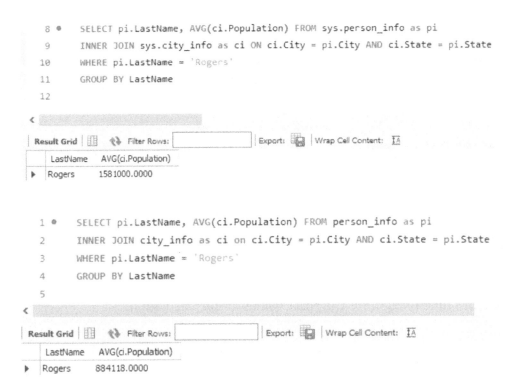

SELECT pi.LastName, AVG(ci.Population) FROM person_info as pi,
This part of the query states what information we would like to retrieve from the database. In this case we would like to know the last name of the person, along with the average of their cities' population.

INNER JOIN city_info as ci ON ci.City = pi.City AND ci.State = pi.State,

We have seen this before. We join our city_info table to our person_info based on matching City and State columns.

WHERE pi.LastName = 'Rogers',

This WHERE clause means we will only retrieve results for individuals with the last name, Rogers.

GROUP BY LastName, the last piece of the puzzle. This groups our results based on the LastName column.

11.4 - SUM()

The SUM function is an aggregate function that allows you to calculate the sum of values in a set. The sum is result of adding two or more numbers. The syntax of the SUM function is as follows:

SUM([DISTINCT] expression)
Note the [DISTINCT] is optional.

If you use the SUM function in a SELECT statement that returns no row, the SUM function returns NULL, not zero. The DISTINCT option instructs the SUM function to calculate the sum of only the distinct values in a set.

The SUM function ignores the NULL values in the calculation.

Let's see the SUM syntax in action by looking at a practical example:

```
1  •    SELECT SUM(Population) from person_info as pi
2       INNER JOIN city_info as ci ON ci.City = pi.City AND ci.State = pi.State
3
```

SUM(Population)
4183026

SELECT SUM(Population), this stipulates that we want the sum of the population column.

FROM person_info as pi, we are taking this information from the person_info table.

INNER JOIN city_info as ci ON ci.City = pi.City AND ci.State = pi.State,

We must join the city_info data as this contains the data that we want. We join this based on matching City and State column values.

> Give It A Try! First, use GROUP BY to confirm that three people have the same last name. Use the COUNT() function with a join to determine how many people have a population associated with their hometown. Of those people, determine both the total and average populations.

11.5 - ORDER BY

When you use the SELECT statement to retrieve data from a table, the result set is not sorted by default. This means that the rows in the result set can be returned in any order.

To sort the result set, you add the ORDER BY clause to the SELECT statement. The syntax of the ORDER BY statement is as follows:

```
SELECT
    select_list
FROM
    table_name
ORDER BY
    column_1 [ASC|DESC],
    column_2 [ASC|DESC],
    ...
```

In this syntax, you can specify one or more columns which you want to sort after the ORDER BY clause.

The ASC stands for ascending and the DESC stands for descending. You can use ASC to sort the result set in ascending order and DESC to sort the result set in descending order.

This ORDER BY clause sorts the result set in ascending order:

ORDER BY column_1 ASC;

And this ORDER BY clause sorts the result set in descending order:

ORDER BY column_1 DESC;

By default, the ORDER BY clause uses ASC, and sorts the result if you don't explicitly specify any option.

Therefore, the following clauses are equivalent:

ORDER BY column_1 ASC;
and
ORDER BY column_1;

If you want to sort the result set by multiple columns, you specify a comma-separated list of columns in the ORDER BY clause:

ORDER BY
    column_1,
    column_2;

It's also possible to sort the results by a column in ascending order, and then by another column in descending order:

ORDER BY
    column1 ASC,
    column2 DESC;

In this case, for the ORDER BY clause:

- The result set gets sorted based on the values in column_1. Then the same result set gets sorted by column_2 in descending order.
- Note that the order of values in the column1 will not change in this step, only the order of values in the column_2 changes.
- Note that the ORDER BY clause is always evaluated after the FROM and SELECT clause.

Chapter 12: Subqueries/Nested Queries

12.1 - What is a subquery?

A subquery is a select query that is contained inside another query. The inner select query is usually used to determine the results of the outer select query.

Subqueries are embedded queries inside another query. The embedded query is known as the inner query, and the container query is known as the outer query. Subqueries are easy to use, offer great flexibility, and can be easily broken down into single logical components making up the query. This makes debugging and testing these types of queries very simple.

MySQL supports three types of subqueries, scalar, row, and table subqueries:
1. Scalar sub queries only return a single row and single column.
2. Row sub queries only return a single row but can have more than one column.
3. Table subqueries can return multiple rows as well as columns.

Subqueries can also be used in INSERT, UPDATE and DELETE queries.

For performance issues, when it comes to getting data from multiple tables, it's strongly recommended to use JOINs instead of subqueries. Subqueries should only be used with good reason.

12.2 - Subqueries vs. JOIN

When compared with JOIN, subqueries are simple to use and easy to read. They are not as complicated as JOIN, making them frequently used by beginners. However, subqueries often suffer from performance issues, with all varieties of the JOIN command offering a much better performance.

Given a choice, it is recommended to use a JOIN over a subquery.

Subqueries should only be used as a last resort when you cannot use a JOIN operation to achieve the desired outcome.

One of the challenges in writing SQL queries is choosing whether to use a subquery or a JOIN. There are many situations in which a JOIN is the better solution, and there are others where a subquery is better. Let's consider this topic in detail.

Subqueries are used in complex SQL queries. Usually, there is a main outer query, and one or more subqueries nested within the outer query. Subqueries can be simple or correlated. Simple subqueries do not rely on the columns in the outer query, where correlated subqueries refer to data from the outer query.

Let's identify the key differences between an inner and outer query.

12.3 - Inner Query

A subquery can be defined as one query embedded in another query. A normal SQL query divided into two parts. One part is the inner query and the other part is the outer query. The inner query is called a subquery, which is placed in the round parentheses (or brackets), after the WHERE or FROM clause.

12.4 - Outer Query

The outer query gets executed after the subquery generates a result that is used by the outer query to produce the output. Comparison operators such as: $<,>,=,\leq,=<,\geq$ can be used in the subquery to compare both queries and give an output. The subquery must be placed on the right side of the expression operator.

Correlated Subquery is a type of subquery that is often used in tandem with an outer query. Correlated Subqueries are different from the normal subquery in terms of execution. In this query, the correlated subquery is evaluated once for each row of the outer query. A correlated subquery is slower compared to a normal subquery.

Let's look at a quick example to show how correlated subqueries relate to outer queries:

In a SQL database query, a correlated subquery (also known as a synchronized subquery) is a subquery (a query nested inside another query) that uses values from the outer query. Because the subquery may be evaluated once for each row processed by the outer query, it can be slow.

Here is an example for a typical correlated subquery. In this example, the objective is to find all employees whose salary is above average for their department.

Let's apply this to a practical example. Imagine our person_info table has a column called 'Age' which contains data regarding the age of each person.

```
SELECT FirstName, LastName, Age
   FROM person_info pi
   WHERE Age > (
      SELECT AVG(Age)
         FROM person_info
         WHERE PersonID = pi.PersonID);
```

In the above query the outer query is:

```
SELECT FirstName, LastName, Age
FROM person_info pi
WHERE Age > ...
```

and the inner query (the correlated subquery) is

```
SELECT AVG(Age)
FROM person_info
WHERE PersonID = pi.PersonID
```

A JOIN is more efficient in most cases, but there are cases in which constructs other than a subquery are not possible. While subqueries may be more readable for beginners, JOINs are more readable for experienced SQL coders as the queries become more complex. It is a good practice to avoid multiple levels of nested subqueries, since they are not easily readable and do not have good performance.

In general, it's better to write a query with JOINs, rather than with subqueries if possible, especially if the subqueries are correlated.

> Give It A Try! Use a subquery to list the names of people whose hometowns have a population greater than 500,000. Try doing so with a subquery and not a join.
>
> The solution is below:

```
 8 •    SELECT FirstName, LastName FROM person_info as pi
 9      WHERE City in
10      (SELECT City FROM city_info WHERE Population > 500000)
11
12
```

Result Grid | Filter Rows: | Export: | Wrap Cell Content:

FirstName	LastName
Jack	Rogers
Alexandra	Howard

Chapter 13: Control Flow Tools

13.1 - The CASE Function

The CASE function is a control flow tool that allows you to add if-else logic to a query. Generally speaking, you can use the CASE expression anywhere that allows a valid expression. For example, with SELECT, WHERE, and ORDER BY clauses.

The CASE statement goes through conditions and returns a value when the first condition is met (like an IF-THEN-ELSE statement). So, once a condition is true, it will stop reading and return the result.

If no conditions are true, it will return the value in the ELSE clause.

If there isn't an ELSE part and no conditions are true, it returns NULL.

The CASE expression has two forms: simple CASE and searched CASE.

Below is the syntax for the CASE expression:

```
CASE value
    WHEN value_1 THEN result_1
    WHEN value_2 THEN result_2
    ...
    [ELSE else_result]
END
```

In this syntax, CASE matches the value with the value_1, value_2, checking to see if the values are equal, if a match is found, it returns the corresponding result_1, or result_2.

If the value does not equal to any value_1, or value_2, CASE returns the result in the ELSE clause if the ELSE clause is specified.

The CASE compares the value with values in the WHEN clauses for equality, you cannot use it with NULL because NULL = NULL returns false.

The CASE expression returns a result whose data type depends on the context where it is used. For example, if the CASE expression is used in the character string context, it returns the result as a character string. If the CASE expression is used in a numeric context, it returns the result as an integer, a decimal, or a real value.

Let's apply this information to a practical example. Say we want to show whether the states in our State column in the person_info table is in the east, west or central part of the country. How would we achieve this?

```
SELECT *,
    CASE STATE WHEN 'PA' THEN 'EAST'
    WHEN 'MD' THEN 'EAST'
    WHEN 'DC' THEN 'EAST'
    WHEN 'WA' THEN 'WEST'
    WHEN 'OH' THEN 'CENTRAL'
    WHEN 'OR' THEN 'WEST'
    WHEN 'NM' THEN 'WEST'
    WHEN 'NY' THEN 'EAST'
    WHEN 'AZ' THEN 'WEST'
    WHEN 'KS' THEN 'CENTRAL'
    END AS region
  from person_info
```

SELECT *, we have seen this before. We want to show everything that is currently in the table.

CASE STATE WHEN 'PA' THEN 'EAST', we introduce our CASE function here.

You can see that WHEN the State is equal to 'PA' (Pennsylvania), then we want to assign the value of 'EAST,' as this state is on the eastern side of the country.

We continue this pattern for the rest of the states in our table. For example, WHEN 'KS' THEN 'CENTRAL.'

END AS region, this is an important line in our SQL query. This assigns the values of EAST/WEST/CENTRAL to appear under this new column, which will be showed as region. This does not create a column called 'region' permanently. It is just there to show the results of the values. If you use SELECT * on the person_info table once more, you will not see the region column.

Here is the output of the previous example:

PersonID	FirstName	LastName	Gender	City	State	region
1	Jack	Rogers	Male	Philadelphia	PA	EAST
2	John	Rogers	Male	Baltimore	MD	EAST
3	Hollie	Rogers	Female	Washington	DC	EAST
4	Ralph	Levin	Male	Seattle	WA	WEST
5	Paul	Harrison	Male	Columbus	OH	CENTRAL
6	Sandra	Dobkin	Female	Eugene	OR	WEST
7	Linda	Flowers	Unknown	Albuquerque	NM	WEST
8	Ruth	Smith	Female	Ithaca	NY	EAST
9	Alexandra	Howard	Female	Tucson	AZ	WEST
10	Alan	Miller	Male	Topeka	KS	CENTRAL

Give It A Try! Use the CASE function to create an additional column that gives the region as 'East,' 'West,' or 'Central' based on the state listed.

13.2 - The IF Function

The MySQL IF function is used for validating a condition. The IF function returns a value if the condition is TRUE and another value if the condition is FALSE. The IF function can return values that can be either numeric or a string depending on the context in which the function is used.

The IF function accepts one parameter, which is the condition to be evaluated.

The syntax for the IF function:

IF(condition, true_value, false_value)

condition -- It is used to specify the condition to be evaluated.

true_value – It is an optional parameter, which is used to specify the value to be returned if the condition evaluates to be true.

false_value – It is an optional parameter, which is used to specify the value to be returned if the condition evaluates to be false.

Return Value:

The IF function returns a value if the condition is TRUE or a different value if the condition is FALSE.

Let's apply this new knowledge regarding the IF function to a practical example. Look at the SQL query below:

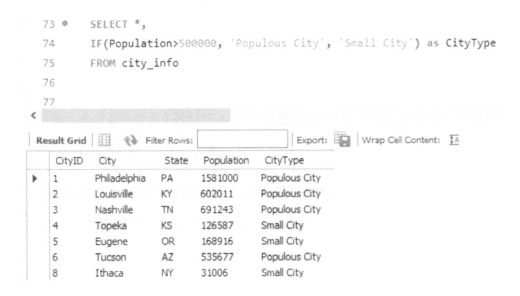

SELECT *, we want to retrieve all the records from our city_info table.

IF(Population>500000, 'Populous City', 'Small City') as CityType

Let's breakdown this IF statement:

- Population > 500000, this is the value we are checking. We are checking if the value of the Population exceeds 500,000.
- 'Populous City,' 'Small City,' if the value in the Population column does indeed exceed 500,000; we take the value on the left, Populous City.

- If the value in the Population column **does not** indeed exceed 500,000; we take the value on the right, Small City.
- As CityType, the result of our IF function will be stored under this heading of CityType.

FROM city_info, this data is being taken from our city_info table.

Give It A Try! Use the IF function to create an additional column CityType that marks the cities in city_info as a populous city (if the population is greater than 500,000) or a small city otherwise.

Chapter 14: Views, Stored Procedures, and Triggers

14.1 - Views

Views are virtual tables that do not store any data of their own, but display data stored in other tables. In other words, Views are essentially a special type of SQL query. A view can contain all or several rows from a table. A MySQL View can show data from one table or many tables.

A view provides several benefits.

1. Views can hide complexity.
   If you have a query that requires joining several tables, or has complex logic or calculations, you can code all of the logic into a view, then select from the view just like you would a table.

2. Views can be used as a security mechanism.
   A view can select certain columns and/or rows from a table (or tables), and permissions set on the view, instead of the underlying tables. This allows surfacing only the data that a user needs to see.

3. Views can simplify supporting legacy code.
   If you need to re-factor a table that would break a lot of code, you can replace the table with a view of the same name. The view provides the exact same schema as the original table, while the actual schema has changed. This keeps the legacy code that references the table from breaking, allowing you to change the legacy code at your leisure.

These are just some of the many examples of how views can be useful. Let's look at how we go about creating views.

While views do provide some advantages, we also must mention some of the potential drawbacks users may face when using views.

1. Views that hide complexity, nested views (views that are called by another view), or views with complex joins can be a source of unexpected performance problems.

2. Views can hide bugs when rebuilds or updates change underlying tables. Views can unexpectedly change. These changes can produce problems in areas of the code which are not immediately flagged as needing modifications. This is due to the detail that they were indirectly referencing through the modified tables rather than directly referencing the tables.

3. Views themselves have a performance cost that the user should be aware of.

While views can be powerful tool in your arsenal, like any powerful tool, they can be dangerous if misused.

The CREATE VIEW statement creates a new view in the database.

Here is the basic syntax of the CREATE VIEW statement:

```
CREATE [OR REPLACE] VIEW [database_name.]view_name [(column_list)]
AS
   select_statement;
```

In this syntax:

First, specify the name of the view that you want to create after the CREATE VIEW keywords. The name of the view must be unique in a database. Since views and tables in the same database share the same namespace, the name of a view cannot be the same as the name of an existing table.

Second, use the OR REPLACE option if you want to replace an existing view if the view already exists. If the view does not exist, the OR REPLACE has no effect. This is completely optional when using the CREATE VIEW statement.

Third, specify a list of columns for the view. By default, the columns of the view are derived from the select list of the SELECT statement. However, you can explicitly specify the column list for the view by listing them in parentheses following the view name.

Finally, specify a SELECT statement that defines the view. The SELECT statement can query data from tables or views. MySQL allows you to use the ORDER BY clause in the SELECT statement but ignores it if you select from the view with a query that has its own ORDER BY clause.

By default, the CREATE VIEW statement creates a view in the current database. If you want to explicitly create a view in a given database, you can qualify the view name with the database name.

Let's apply this CREATE VIEW syntax to a practical example:

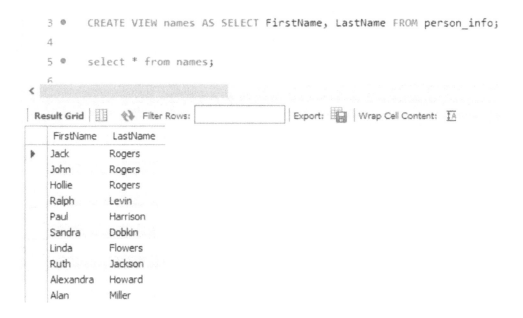

CREATE VIEW names AS, this creates a view called 'names.' We use AS at the end to specify what SQL query this view contains.

SELECT FirstName and LastName FROM person_info, this is the functionality of our view. When used, it will retrieve all the FirstName and LastName data from our person_info table.

129

14.2 - Altering a View

The ALTER VIEW statement changes the definition of an existing view. The syntax of the ALTER VIEW is like the CREATE VIEW statement:

ALTER VIEW view_name [(column_list)]
    AS select_statement;

First, specify the name of the view that you want to alter after the ALTER VIEW keywords.

Second, specify the list of columns you wish to change for the view. By default, the columns of the view are derived from the select list of the SELECT statement. However, you can explicitly specify the column list for the view by listing them in parentheses following the view name.

Finally, specify the new SELECT statement that will replace the old one in the view.

Time to look at a practical example. Please analyze the SQL query below:

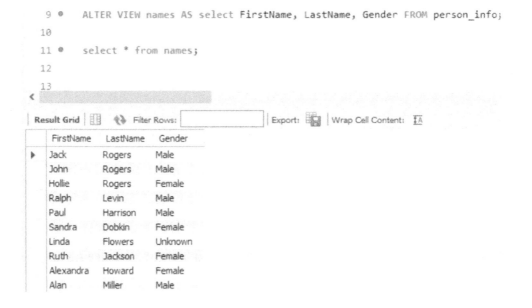

```
9 •    ALTER VIEW names AS select FirstName, LastName, Gender FROM person_info;
10
11 •    select * from names;
12
13
```

FirstName	LastName	Gender
Jack	Rogers	Male
John	Rogers	Male
Hollie	Rogers	Female
Ralph	Levin	Male
Paul	Harrison	Male
Sandra	Dobkin	Female
Linda	Flowers	Unknown
Ruth	Jackson	Female
Alexandra	Howard	Female
Alan	Miller	Male

14.3 - Deleting a View

Deleting a view is a simple task. The syntax for deleting a view is as follows:

DROP VIEW view_name;

If we wanted to delete our previously created view which was called 'names,' we would execute the following query:

```
DROP VIEW names;
```

14.4 - Stored Procedures

A stored procedure is a set of SQL statements with an assigned name, which are stored in a relational DBMS as a group, so it can be reused and shared by multiple programs.

Here are some of the benefits of using a stored procedure:

A stored procedure provides an important layer of security between the user interface and the database. It supports security through data access controls because end users may enter or change data, but do not write procedures. A stored procedure preserves data integrity because information is entered in a consistent manner. It improves productivity because statements in a stored procedure only must be written once.

Stored procedures offer advantages over embedding queries in a graphical user interface (GUI). Since stored procedures are modular, it is easier to troubleshoot when a problem arises in an application. Stored procedures are also tuneable, which eliminates the need to modify the GUI source code to improve its performance. It's easier to code stored procedures than to build a query through a GUI.

The use of stored procedures can reduce network traffic between clients and servers because the commands are executed as a single batch of code. This means only the call to execute the procedure is sent over a network, instead of every single line of code being sent individually.

Stored procedures are often confused with functions. Stored procedures and functions can be used to accomplish the same task. Both can be custom defined as part of any application, but functions are designed to send their output to a query. Stored procedures are designed to return outputs to the application, while a user-defined function returns table variables and cannot change the server environment or operating system environment.

First, you create the stored procedure. Then once it is created, you can run it (or more precisely, you 'call' it).

When you call a stored procedure, you also provide any parameters that it might require. The stored procedure will then execute, using your parameters in any way that the code specifies.

For example, you can write a stored procedure that accepts the PersonID parameter. The stored procedure can then take that parameter and use it to check the person_info table for that particular person. Therefore, you can call the stored procedure, each time with a different PersonID, and it would perform an action to that person.

To create a stored procedure, we must use the CREATE PROCEDURE statement.

The syntax for creating a stored procedure is as follows:

```
DELIMITER //

CREATE PROCEDURE sp_name(parameter_1 INT)
BEGIN
   ... The code for your stored procedure goes here...
END;

DELIMITER ;
```

Replace sp_name with whatever name you'd like to use for the stored procedure. The parentheses are required, they enclose any parameters. If no parameters are required, the parentheses can be empty.

The main body of the stored procedure goes in between the BEGIN and END keywords. These keywords are used for writing compound statements. A compound statement can contain multiple statements, and these can be nested if required. Therefore, you can nest BEGIN and END blocks.

In most cases, you will also need to surround the CREATE PROCEDURE statement with DELIMITER commands and change END; to END //.

In the above example, we added a couple of DELIMITER commands and we replaced a semicolon with two forward slashes. What's going on here?

We did this to tell MySQL to use a different delimiter while it creates our stored procedure.

The reason for this is that MySQL already recognizes the semicolon as a delimiter for marking the end of each SQL statement. Therefore, as soon as MySQL sees the first semicolon, it will interpret the delimiter as such, and our stored procedure would break.

The DELIMITER command allows us to tell MySQL to use a different delimiter. In the above example we set this to two forward slashes (//), but this could have been anything (although, avoid using a backslash (\) as that is the escape character for MySQL). By changing the delimiter, MySQL won't try to interpret our semicolons as the end of the statement, it will wait until it sees the two forward slashes.

Once we have created the stored procedure, we can use DELIMITER to reset the delimiter back to the semicolon.

Let's apply this information to an example:

```
DELIMITER //

●    CREATE PROCEDURE Locations()
     BEGIN
         SELECT City, State FROM person_info;
     END //


DELIMITER ;
```

- DELIMITER //, We initialize our DELIMITER to be '//' before we do anything else.
- CREATE PROCEDURE Locations(), this creates a stored procedure called 'Locations.'
- BEGIN, this tells MySQL that the following statements will make up our stored procedure.
- SELECT City, State FROM person_info, when we call our stored procedure MySQL will execute this query.
- END //, this tells MySQL we have finished defining our stored procedure.

Now that we have defined our stored procedure, how do we execute, or call it? It is as simple as:

134

As you can see in the Results Grid in the previous image, when the stored procedure was called, it executed SELECT City, State FROM person_info, as expected.

We already mentioned the usefulness of adding parameters to your stored procedures to make them more reusable. Let's look at a practical example of how parameters work. Analyze the image below:

```
28  ●⊖    CREATE PROCEDURE people_by_gender(
29             IN personGender VARCHAR(255)
30       )
31    ⊖ BEGIN
32             SELECT * FROM person_info
33             WHERE Gender = personGender;
34       END //
35       DELIMITER ;
36  ●    Call people_by_gender('Female')
37
```

	PersonID	FirstName	LastName	Gender	City	State
▶	3	Hollie	Rogers	Female	Washington	DC
	6	Sandra	Dobkin	Female	Eugene	OR
	8	Ruth	Jackson	Female	Ithaca	NY
	9	Alexandra	Howard	Female	Tucson	AZ

```
CREATE PROCEDURE people_by_gender(
    IN personGender VARCHAR(255)
)
```

Notice how this CREATE PROCEDURE statement differs from the previous example. The brackets are no longer empty. They contain our parameter. IN means this stored procedure requires a parameter to be supplied when it is called.

personGender VARCHAR(255), our parameter is called 'personGender' and it has the data type of VARCHAR. If you supply a parameter that is of data type INT, or any other data type that is not VARCHAR, MySQL will return an error message.

```
BEGIN
    SELECT * FROM person_info
    WHERE Gender = personGender;
END //
DELIMITER ;
```

As before, we define the action that the stored procedure performs between the BEGIN and END keywords. Note the use of the personGender parameter here.

```
Call people_by_gender('Female');
```

Finally, this is where we call our stored procedure. The parameter provided was the VARCHAR 'Female.' Our stored procedure was defined as:

```
SELECT * FROM person_info
WHERE Gender = personGender;
```

When we provide the parameter 'Female,' the above statement changes to the following:

```
SELECT * FROM person_info
WHERE Gender = 'Female';
```

If we wanted to retrieve the data for where the gender is male, we would simply execute Call people_by_gender('Male'). This is the power of stored procedures.

14.5 - LOOPs

With MySQL, stored procedures can be combined with loops in useful and interesting ways. If you are confused by the term loop, don't worry. Loops are among the most basic and powerful of programming concepts. A loop in a computer program is an instruction that repeats until a specified condition is reached. In a loop structure, the loop asks a question. If the answer requires action, it is executed. The same question is asked again and again until no further action is required. Each time the question is asked is called an iteration.

A computer programmer who needs to use the same lines of code many times in a program can use a loop to save time. Just about every programming language includes the concept of a loop and this includes MySQL.

Take special care when using loops, if the condition is never met, the loop will execute indefinitely until you manually kill the process.

Let's look at a practical example to grain a greater understanding of how stored procedures can be combined with loops in MySQL:

```
78      DELIMITER //
79  ●   CREATE PROCEDURE tens_loop3()
80  ⊖   BEGIN
81          DECLARE counter INT DEFAULT 0;
82  ⊖      my_tens_loop3: LOOP
83          SET counter = counter+10;
84  ⊖      IF counter > 100 THEN
85              LEAVE my_tens_loop3;
86          END IF;
87          select counter;
88          END LOOP my_tens_loop3;
89          END //
```

Result Grid	Filter Rows:	Export:
counter
▶ 100

First, we create a procedure as we have done before by writing CREATE PROCEDURE tens_loop3.

DECLARE counter INT DEFAULT 0, there is a lot to unpack in this statement.

First, you're probably wondering what the DECLARE keyword does. This declares a variable called 'counter.' What is a variable you ask? A variable is a named data object whose value can change during the stored procedure execution. We typically use variables in stored procedures to hold immediate results. These variables are local to the stored procedure.

Before using a variable, you must declare it using the DECLARE keyword.

Second, you are probably wondering about the purpose of the DEFAULT keyword.

The MySQL DEFAULT keyword is a database CONSTRAINT or RULE that is applied when inserting new records into a table. If the value is not provided to any column while inserting a new row in the table, the default value will be used instead.

Why use the MySQL DEFAULT value?

There are benefits of specifying default values in MySQL. In the below cases, we need to set the DEFAULT value.

For most of the data types, MySQL provides 'NULL' as a DEFAULT value. In the case of Primary Key columns, these cannot contain 'NULL' values. In this case, a DEFAULT unique value is a good way to handle this.

For predefined standards or business rules, we can use DEFAULT values instead of manually specifying the field every time. For example, inserting DATETIME values in a DATE column to identify when the record is inserted in a table.

What are the types of DEFAULT values?

1. Implicit: MySQL automatically sets a default value if not provided.

For numeric data types, the default is 0. If a column is declared as an integer and with the AUTO_INCREMENT attribute, the default is the next value in the sequence.

2. Explicit: We can explicitly set a DEFAULT value when creating or altering a table.

Now that you understand the DECLARE and DEFAULT keyword, time to go back to our looping stored procedure:

```
DECLARE counter INT DEFAULT 0.
```

We now know that this defines a variable called counter, and the default value of this variable is 0.

my_tens_loop3: LOOP, this tells MySQL that this is the start of our loop.

SET counter = counter+10; this assigns the value of our variable to be the current value plus ten. For example, on the first iteration of our loop this expression evaluates to SET counter = 0 + 10. On the second iteration, it becomes SET counter 10+10 and so forth.

```
IF counter > 100 THEN
    LEAVE my_tens_loop3;
END IF
```

This IF statement checks the current value of our loop. If the current value is greater than 100, then we use the LEAVE keyword to exit our LOOP immediately. Any SQL commands following this LEAVE keyword will not be executed in this case.

SELECT counter, this selects the current value of our loop.

END LOOP, this ends our loop. After this command, we jump back to the start of the loop and iterate through it. This will keep happening until we instruct MySQL to leave our loop using the LEAVE keyword.

There are more types of loops and control flow statements.

14.6 - WHILE

The WHILE statement is another type of loop. The WHILE loop will keep looping as a specific condition is met. Be careful when using this statement, if the condition is never met, the WHILE loop will execute indefinitely until you manually kill the process.

The syntax for the WHILE statement in MySQL is:

```
WHILE condition DO
    {
        code
    }
END WHILE;
```

condition – The condition is tested with each iteration of the WHILE loop. If the condition evaluates to be TRUE, the loop body is executed. If the condition evaluates to be FALSE, the WHILE loop is terminated.

code – The statements of code to execute with each iteration of the WHILE loop.

You usually use a WHILE loop statement when you are unsure of how many times you want the loop body to execute. Since the WHILE condition is evaluated before entering the loop, it is possible that the loop body may not execute even once.

Let's apply the syntax for the WHILE loop statement to a practical example:

```
1       DELIMITER //
2   ●   CREATE PROCEDURE while_example()
3   ⊝   BEGIN
4           DECLARE counter INT DEFAULT 0;
5
6   ⊝       WHILE counter < 100 DO
7
8           SET counter = counter + 10;
9           SELECT counter;
10
11  ├       END WHILE;
12  └       END //
13      DELIMITER ;
```

WHILE counter < 100 DO, here we initialize the WHILE loop. Look at the condition, counter < 100. This means we want to execute the code inside of the WHILE loop as long as the value of counter is less than 100.

SET counter = counter+10; This assigns the value of our variable to be the current value plus ten. For example, on the first iteration of our loop this expression evaluates to SET counter = 0 + 10. On the second iteration it becomes SET counter 10+10 and so forth.

SELECT counter; We want to select the current value of counter on each iteration of the WHILE loop.

END WHILE; Once MySQL reaches this point; it will jump back to check the condition (counter < 100) and execute the code again if this condition is met.

14.7 - REPEAT

Another type of loop can be achieved through the use of the REPEAT statement. The REPEAT statement is used when you do not know how many times you want the loop body to execute. It provides a similar functionality to the WHILE loop (discussed later).

Syntax

The syntax for the REPEAT statement in MySQL is:

```
REPEAT
    { code_to_execute }
UNTIL condition

END REPEAT [ label_name ];
```

code_to_execute – The statements of code to execute each pass through the REPEAT loop.

condition – The condition that will terminate the REPEAT loop. The code will keep executing until this condition is met.

You would use a REPEAT statement when you are unsure of how many times you want the loop body to execute. You terminate a REPEAT statement with the UNTIL condition.

Let's look at an example that shows how to use the REPEAT statement in MySQL:

```
DELIMITER //

DECLARE num INT;

SET num= 0;

REPEAT
    SET num= num + 10;
UNTIL num > 100

END REPEAT;

END; //

DELIMITER ;
```

In this MySQL LOOP example, the REPEAT statement would repeat the loop until num is greater than 100, at which point the REPEAT loop would terminate.

14.8 - IF THEN ELSE

The IF-THEN-ELSE statement is used to execute code when a condition is TRUE or execute different code if the condition is evaluated to be FALSE. This can be used if we wish to check more than one condition with our IF statement.

The syntax for using IF THEN ELSE is as follows:

```
IF condition_1 THEN
    { code to execute }
ELSEIF condition_2 THEN
    { different code to execute}
ELSE
    { different code to execute}

END IF;
```

ELSEIF – You would use the ELSEIF condition when you want to execute a set of statements when condition_1 is not true, but condtion_2 is true.
ELSE – The code relating to the ELSE condition would only be executed if both condition_1 and condition_2 are evaluated to be false.

Once a condition is found to be TRUE, the IF THEN ELSE statement will execute the corresponding code and not evaluate the conditions any further.

If no condition is met, the ELSE portion of the IF THEN ELSE statement will be executed.

It is important to note that the ELSEIF and ELSE portions are optional and should only be used if using a simple IF statement is not enough.

Let's apply this syntax to a practical example:

```
1     DELIMITER //
2  ●  CREATE PROCEDURE if_else_example()
3  ⊝  BEGIN
4         DECLARE counter INT DEFAULT 0;
5         DECLARE result VARCHAR(256);
6         SET result = "";
7  ⊝      loop_until_thirty: LOOP
8         SET counter = counter + 10;
9  ⊝      IF counter = 10 THEN
10           SET result = "result is 10";
11        ELSEIF counter = 20 THEN
12           SET result = "result is 20";
13        ELSE
14           SET result = "time to leave the loop";
15           LEAVE loop_until_thirty;
16        END IF;
17
18        SELECT counter,result;
19        END LOOP loop_until_thirty;
20     END //
```

DECLARE counter INT DEFAULT 0
DECLARE result VARCHAR(256);

First, we declare two variables. The first is a variable called counter, which has the data type of INT. The second variable is called result and is of type VARCHAR.

SET result = ''; This sets our result value to an empty string.

loop_until_thirty; LOOP, here is the start of our loop.

SET counter = counter+10; This assigns the value of our variable to be the current value plus ten. For example, on the first iteration of our loop this expression evaluates to SET counter = 0 + 10, on the second iteration it becomes SET counter 10+10, and so forth.

```
IF counter = 10 THEN
        SET result = 'result is 10';
```

This is the start of our IF...ELSEIF...ELSE syntax. We check if the value of counter is equal to 10. If this is the case, we set our result to be the string 'result is 10.' After this is evaluated to be true, the ELSEIF and ELSE conditions are skipped.

```
ELSEIF counter = 20 THEN
        SET result = 'result is 20';
```

If the first condition was not met (IF counter = 10), this condition gets checked. If counter has a value of 20, the result gets set to contain the string 'result is 20.'

```
ELSE
        SET result = 'time to leave the loop';
        LEAVE loop_until_thirty;
```

If both conditions that preceded this example were not met (IF counter = 10, ELSEIF counter = 20) the code in this ELSE condition gets executed. In this case, it sets the result to the string value 'time to leave the loop,' as well as using the LEAVE command to leave the current loop_until_thirty loop.

14.9 - Triggers

In MySQL, a trigger is a stored program invoked automatically in response to an event such as insert, update, or delete that occurs in the associated table. For example, you can define a trigger that is invoked automatically before a new row is inserted into a table.

MySQL supports triggers that are invoked in response to the INSERT, UPDATE, or DELETE event.

The SQL standard defines two types of triggers: row-level triggers and statement-level triggers.

145

A row-level trigger is activated for each row that is inserted, updated, or deleted. For example, if a table has 100 rows inserted, updated, or deleted, the trigger is automatically invoked 100 times for the 100 rows affected.

A statement-level trigger is executed once for each transaction regardless of how many rows are inserted, updated, or deleted.

MySQL supports only row-level triggers, it doesn't support statement-level triggers.

Triggers are generally used for auditing purposes and specifically, before and after data change auditing. Triggers can guard against accidental or incorrect INSERT, UPDATE, and DELETE operations.

Triggers can be set up easily and track a variety of information. Triggers can be easily customized allowing users to build their own auditing information repositories. Triggers are an intrusive technology and can throw errors to your client applications when they break.

Let's look at how we can create a trigger in MySQL. A trigger is a named database object that is associated with a table, and it activates when a particular event (e.g. an insert, update, or delete) occurs for the table. The statement CREATE TRIGGER creates a new trigger in MySQL. Here is the syntax:

```
CREATE
[DEFINER = { user | CURRENT_USER }]
TRIGGER trigger_name
trigger_time trigger_event
ON table_name FOR EACH ROW
trigger_body
trigger_time: { BEFORE | AFTER }
trigger_event: { INSERT | UPDATE | DELETE }
```

DEFINER clause: The DEFINER clause specifies the MySQL account to be used when checking access privileges at trigger activation time. If a user value is given, it should be a MySQL account specified as 'user_name'@'host_name', CURRENT_USER, or CURRENT_USER().

The default DEFINER value is the user who executes the CREATE TRIGGER statement. This is the same as specifying DEFINER = CURRENT_USER explicitly. If you specify the DEFINER clause, these rules determine the valid DEFINER user values:

- If you do not have the SUPER privilege, the only permitted user value is your own account, either specified literally or by using CURRENT_USER. You cannot set the definer to some other account.
- If you have the SUPER privilege, you can specify any syntactically valid account name. If the account does not actually exist, a warning is shown.
- Although it is possible to create a trigger with a non-existent DEFINER account, it is not a good idea for such triggers to be activated until the account does exist.

trigger_name, all triggers must have unique names within a schema. Triggers in different schemas can have the same name.

trigger_time, this is the trigger action time. It can be BEFORE or AFTER to indicate that the trigger activates before or after each row to be modified.

trigger_event, this indicates the kind of operation that activates the trigger.

These trigger_event values are permitted:

1. The trigger activates whenever a new row is inserted into the table. For example, through INSERT, LOAD DATA, and REPLACE statements.
2. The trigger activates whenever a row is modified; for example, through UPDATE statements.
3. The trigger activates whenever a row is deleted from the table; for example, through DELETE and REPLACE statements. DROP TABLE and TRUNCATE TABLE statements on the table do not activate this trigger because they do not use DELETE. Dropping a partition does not activate DELETE triggers either.

table_name shows that the trigger will be associated with the table named table_name. It must refer to a permanent table. You cannot associate a trigger with a TEMPORARY table or a view.

trigger_body is the statement to execute when the trigger activates. To execute multiple statements, use the BEGIN ... END compound statement construct. This also enables you to use the same statements that are permissible within stored routines.

Let's apply this syntax to a practical example:

```
ALTER TABLE person_info
ADD COLUMN action varchar(255);


CREATE TRIGGER trigger_name
before UPDATE
ON person_info FOR EACH ROW
set NEW.action = 'updated';
```

First, we add a column to our existing person_info table by using the ALTER TABLE command we have covered previously, in combination with a new command. ADD COLUMN does what you would expect. This adds a column to our existing table. In this case, it adds a column called action, which has the data type of VARCHAR.

With our column added, it is time to create our trigger. We do this by writing CREATE TRIGGER trigger_name.

before UPDATE, the trigger time is 'before,' meaning that this trigger will activate before the UPDATE command is called.

ON person_info FOR EACH ROW
Set NEW.action = 'updated'

This relates the trigger we are creating to our person_info table. FOR EACH ROW, makes our trigger activate for each row. As you can see, we set a new value for our action column, setting it to 'updated' each time the trigger activates.

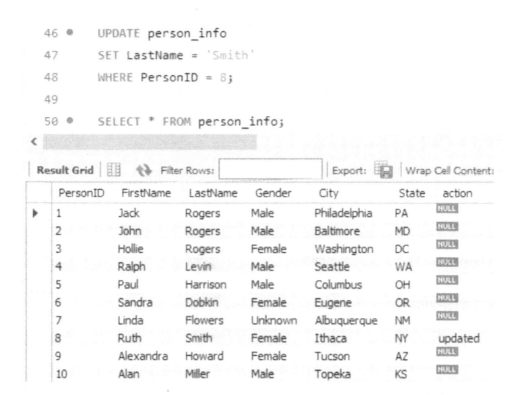

14.10 - DROP TRIGGER

Once you have created a trigger in MySQL, you might find that you need to remove it from the database. You can achieve this with the DROP TRIGGER statement.

The syntax for using the DROP TRIGGER statement is simply:

DROP TRIGGER trigger_name;

Chapter 15: String Functions

MySQL provides an excellent array of functions, which allows us to precisely manipulate strings. By using these functions, you can perform a large variety of different actions with strings to achieve your desired outcome. You can achieve exactly the result set you want by employing these different techniques.

15.1 - LENGTH

The MySQL LENGTH function returns the length of the specified string. This may be useful if you want to check the length of a value before inserting it into your database.

The syntax for LENGTH is as follows:

LENGTH (string)

string- The string to return the length for.

When using the LENGTH function, a multi-byte character is counted as more than one byte.

Here are some examples of how to use LENGTH:

SELECT LENGTH('Hello');
Result: 5

SELECT LENGTH(' ');
Result: 1

SELECT LENGTH(NULL);
Result: NULL

SELECT LENGTH('');
Result: 0

15.2 - CONCAT

The MySQL CONCAT joins (concatenates) strings together to make a single string. This may be useful if you want to combine strings together from different fields.

The syntax for CONCAT is as follows:

CONCAT(expression1, expression2, ... expression_n)

expression1, expression2, ... expression_n - The expressions to concatenate together.

If expression is a numeric value, it will be converted by the CONCAT function to a binary string.

If all expressions are nonbinary strings, the CONCAT function will return a nonbinary string.

If any of the expressions is a binary string, the CONCAT function will return a binary string.

If any of the expressions is a NULL, the CONCAT function will return a NULL value.

Here are some examples of how to use CONCAT:

SELECT CONCAT('how', 'to', 'join', 'words');
Result: 'howtojoinwords'

SELECT CONCAT('The number is ', 24);
Result: 'The number is 24'

SELECT CONCAT('The result is ', 10+10);
Result: 'The result is 20'

SELECT CONCAT('any value', NULL);
Result: NULL

You can also concatenate expressions together in MySQL by placing the strings next to each other.

For example:
SELECT 'how', 'to', 'join', 'words';
Result: 'howtojoinwords'

SELECT 'The number is ' '24';
Result: 'The number is 24'

SELECT 'The result is ' '10+10';
Result: 'The result is 10+10'

Using the above method of concatenation, each of the expressions must be a string.

15.3 - FORMAT

The MySQL FORMAT function formats a number into the specific format that you want, rounding it to a certain number of decimal places, and then it returns the result as a string.

The syntax for FORMAT is as follows:

FORMAT(number, decimal_places)

number - The number to format.
decimal_places - The number of decimal places to round the number to.

If decimal_places is 0, then the FORMAT function returns a string with no decimal places.

Here are some examples of how to use FORMAT:

SELECT FORMAT(12345.6789, 2);
Result: '12,345.68'

SELECT FORMAT(12345.6789, 0);
Result: '12,346'

SELECT FORMAT(12345.6789, 1);
Result: '12,345.7'

15.4 - INSERT

The MySQL INSERT function inserts a substring into an existing string at a specified position for a certain number of characters.

The syntax for INSERT is as follows:

INSERT(string, position, number, substring)

string – The string to modify.
position – The position in string to insert substring.
number – The number of characters to replace in string.
substring – The substring to insert into string.

The first position in string is 1.

If position is not within the length of string, the INSERT function will return string.

If a number is not within the length of the rest of the string, the INSERT function will replace string starting from position until the end of string.

Here are some examples of how to use INSERT:
SELECT INSERT('hellothere.com', 1, 10, 'goodbyenow');
Result: goodbyenow.com'

SELECT INSERT('hellothere.com', 99, 12, 'goodbyenow');
Result: 'hellothere.com'
SELECT INSERT('abcgh', 4, 2, 'def');
Result: 'abcdef'

15.5 - LEFT

The MySQL LEFT function allows you to extract a substring from a string, starting from the left-most character.

The syntax for LEFT is as follows:

LEFT(string, number_of_characters)

string – The string that you wish to extract from.
number_of_characters – The number of characters that you wish to extract from string starting from the left-most character.

If number_of_characters exceeds the length of string, the LEFT function will return string.

Here are some examples of how to use LEFT:
SELECT LEFT('Hello', 1);
Result: 'H'

SELECT LEFT('HelloThere', 5);
Result: 'Hello'

SELECT LEFT('HelloThereGoodbyeNow', 10);
Result: 'HelloThere'

SELECT LEFT('HelloThereGoodbyeNow', 100);
Result: 'HelloThereGoodbyeNow'

15.6 - RIGHT

The MySQL RIGHT function allows you to extract a substring from a string, starting from the right-most character. It performs the same functionality as the LEFT function, however starting from the opposite side.

The syntax for RIGHT is as follows:

RIGHT(string, number_of_characters)

string – The string that you wish to extract from.
number_of_characters – The number of characters that you wish to extract from string starting from the right-most character.

If number_of_characters exceeds the length of string, the RIGHT function will return string.

Here are some examples of how to use RIGHT:
SELECT RIGHT('Hello', 1);
Result: 'o'

SELECT RIGHT('HelloThere', 5);
Result: 'There'

SELECT RIGHT('HelloThereGoodbyeNow', 10);
Result: 'GoodbyeNow'

SELECT RIGHT('HelloThereGoodbyeNow', 100);
Result: 'HelloThereGoodbyeNow'

15.7 - MID

The MySQL MID function allows you to extract a substring from a string.

The syntax for MID is as follows:

MID(string, start_position, length)

string – The source string used to extract from.
start_position - The position to begin extraction. The first position in the string is always 1.
length – The number of characters to extract.

The first position in string is 1. The index does not start at 0.

If start_position is a positive number, then the MID function starts from the beginning of the string.

If start_position is a negative number, then the MID function starts from the end of the string and counts backwards.

Here are some examples of how to use MID:
SELECT MID('Hello', 3, 2);
Result: 'lo'

mysql> SELECT MID('Hello', 1, 3);
Result: 'Hel'

mysql> SELECT MID('HelloThere', -3, 3);
Result: 'ere'

15.8 - SUBSTRING

Description
The MySQL SUBSTRING function allows you to extract a substring from a string.

Syntax
The syntax for the SUBSTRING function in MySQL is:

string – The string you want to get a section of.
start_position – The position for extraction. The first position in the string is always 1.

length – This is an optional parameter. It is the number of characters to extract. If this parameter is omitted, the SUBSTRING function will return the entire remaining string.

The first position in string is 1. The index does not start at 0.
If start_position is a positive number, then the SUBSTRING function starts from the beginning of the string.

If start_position is a negative number, then the SUBSTRING function starts from the end of the string and counts backwards. Negative values for the start_position parameter was introduced in MySQL 4.1.

The MID function is a synonym of the SUBSTRING function and these can be used interchangeably

Here are some examples of how to use TRIM:
SELECT SUBSTRING('Hello', 4);
Result: 'lo'

SELECT SUBSTRING('Hello' FROM 4);
Result: 'lo'

SELECT SUBSTRING('Hello',1, 4);
Result: 'Hell'

SELECT SUBSTRING('Hello' FROM 1 FOR 4);
Result: 'Hell'

SELECT SUBSTRING('HelloThere', FROM -3 FOR 3);
Result: 'ere'

15.9 - TRIM

The MySQL TRIM function removes all specified characters either from the beginning or the end of a string.

The syntax for TRIM is as follows:

TRIM([LEADING | TRAILING | BOTH] [trim_character FROM] string)

LEADING – This is an optional parameter. Removes the trim_character from the front of string.

TRAILING – This is an optional parameter. Removes the trim_character from the end of string.

BOTH – This is an optional parameter. Removes the trim_character from the front and end of string.

trim_character FROM – This is an optional parameter. The character that will be removed from string. If this parameter is omitted, it will remove space characters from the string.

string – The string to trim.

If you do not specify a value for the first parameter (LEADING, TRAILING, BOTH), the TRIM function will default to BOTH and remove the trim_character from both the front and end of string.

If you do not specify a trim_character, the TRIM function will default the character to be removed as a space character. When most people think about using the TRIM function it is in this context, TRIM is usually used to remove leading and trailing whitespace from a string.

Here are some examples of how to use TRIM:
SELECT TRIM(LEADING ' ' FROM '   HelloThere   ');
Result: 'HelloThere   '

SELECT TRIM(TRAILING ' ' FROM '   HelloThere   ');
Result: '   HelloThere'
SELECT TRIM(BOTH ' ' FROM '   HelloThere   ');
Result: 'HelloThere'

SELECT TRIM(' ' FROM '   HelloThere   ');
Result: HelloThere'

SELECT TRIM('   HelloThere   ');
Result: 'HelloThere'

SELECT TRIM(LEADING '0' FROM '000123');
Result: '123'

SELECT TRIM(TRAILING '1' FROM 'Hello1');
Result: 'Hello'

SELECT TRIM(BOTH '123' FROM '123Hello123');
Result: 'Hello'

15.10 - LTRIM

The MySQL LTRIM function removes all space characters from the left-hand side of a string.

The syntax for LTRIM is as follows:

LTRIM (string)
string – The string to trim the space characters from the left-hand side.

Here are some examples of how to use LTRIM:

SELECT LTRIM('   HelloThere');
Result: 'HelloThere'
SELECT LTRIM('   Hello   how   are   you   ');
Result: 'Hello   how   are   you   '

15.11 - RTRIM

The MySQL RTRIM function removes all space characters from the right-hand side of a string. It performs the same functionality as LTRIM; however, it performs this action to the opposite side of the string.

The syntax for RTRIM is as follows:

RTRIM (string)
string – The string to trim the space characters from the left-hand side.

Here are some examples of how to use RTRIM:

SELECT RTRIM ('HelloThere   ');

Result: 'HelloThere   '

SELECT RTRIM ('   Hello   how   are   you   ');
Result: '   Hello   how   are   you'

15.12 - UPPER

The MySQL UPPER function converts all characters in the specified string to uppercase. If there are characters in the string that are not letters, they are unaffected by this function.

The syntax for UPPER is as follows:

UPPER(string)

string – The string to convert to uppercase.

The UPPER function will convert the characters using the current character mapping set, which is latin1, by default. The UCASE function is a synonym for the UPPER function.

Here are some examples of how to use UPPER:

SELECT UPPER(Hello how are You);
Result: 'HELLO HOW ARE YOU'

SELECT UPPER('hello there   123');
Result: 'HELLO THERE   123 '

15.13 - LOWER

The MySQL LOWER function converts all characters in the specified string to lowercase. If there are characters in the string that are not letters, they are unaffected by this function. This function can be viewed as an opposite to UPPER.

The syntax for LOWER is as follows:

LOWER (string)

string – The string to convert to lowercase.

The LOWER function will convert the characters using the current character mapping set, which is latin1, by default. The LCASE function is a synonym for the LOWER function.

Here are some examples of how to use LOWER:

SELECT LOWER(Hello how are You);
Result: 'hello how are you'

SELECT UPPER(HELLO THERE   123');
Result: 'hello there   123 '

Chapter 16: Numerical Functions

16.1 – ABS

The MySQL ABS function returns the absolute value of a number. The 'absolute value' removes any negative sign in front of a number and evaluates all numbers as positive (or zero).

The syntax for ABS is as follows:

ABS(number)

number – The number to convert to an absolute value.

Here are some examples of how to use ABS:

SELECT ABS(-30);
Result: 30

SELECT ABS(-30.5);
Result: 30.5

SELECT ABS(-35.44);
Result: 35.44

SELECT ABS(35.44);
Result: 35.44

SELECT ABS(30 * -1);
Result: 30

16.2 – CEILING

The MySQL CEILING function returns the smallest integer value that is greater than or equal to a number.

The syntax for CEILING is as follows:

CEILING(number)

number – The value used to find the smallest integer value.

The CEIL function is a synonym for the CEILING function.

Here are some examples of how to use CEILING:

SELECT CEILING(10.75);
Result: 11

SELECT CEILING(10.1);
Result: 11

SELECT CEILING(10);
Result: 10

SELECT CEILING(-10.75);
Result: -10

SELECT CEILING(-10.1);
Result: -10

SELECT CEILING(-10);
Result: -10

16.3 – FLOOR

The MySQL FLOOR function returns the largest integer value that is equal to or less than a number. This function can be viewed as an opposite to the CEILING function.

The syntax for CEILING is as follows:

FLOOR(number)

number – The value used to find the largest integer value.

Here are some examples of how to use FLOOR:

SELECT FLOOR(10.75);
Result: 10

SELECT FLOOR(10.1);
Result: 10

SELECT FLOOR(10);
Result: 10

SELECT FLOOR(-10.75);
Result: -11

SELECT FLOOR(-10.1);
Result: -11

SELECT FLOOR(-10);
Result: -10

16.4 – ROUND

The MySQL ROUND function returns a number rounded to a certain number of decimal places.

The syntax for ROUND is as follows:

ROUND(number, [decimal_places])

number – The number to round.
decimal_places – The number of decimal places to round. This value must be a positive or negative integer. If this parameter is omitted, the ROUND function will round the number to 0 decimal places.

ROUND always returns a value. If decimal_places is negative and larger than the number of digits before the decimal point, ROUND returns 0.

Here are some examples of how to use ROUND:

mysql> SELECT ROUND(10.455);

Result: 10

mysql> SELECT ROUND(10.415, 0);
Result: 125

mysql> SELECT ROUND(10.415, 1);
Result: 10.4

mysql> SELECT ROUND(10.415, 2);
Result: 10.42

mysql> SELECT ROUND(-10.415);
Result: -10

mysql> SELECT ROUND(-10.615);
Result: -11

16.5 - MOD

The MySQL MOD function returns the remainder of n divided by m. MOD stands for modulus. You may not have encountered a modulus operator before if you are new to programming.

Use the MOD function to get the remainder of two numbers, when one is divided by the other. For example, 12 MOD 5 would be equal to 2. The MOD function is useful for situations where you need a fixed number of rows, and would like to know the amount of rows left over. Imagine you had an online store that shows 10 products per page. Now imagine there were 18 products. You could use the MOD function to ensure that you only retrieved the remaining 8 products when the user navigated to the second page of results.

The syntax for MOD is as follows:

n MOD m

OR

MOD(n, m)

OR

n % m (note: % is the operator for MOD)

All three of the above syntax are valid.

n – The value that will be divided by m.
m – The value that will be divided into n.

Here are some examples of how to use MOD:

SELECT MOD(12, 5);
Result: 2

SELECT 12 % 5;
Result: 2

16.6 - SQRT

The MySQL SQRT function returns the square root of a number.

The syntax for SQRT is as follows:

SQRT(number)
Parameters or Arguments
number – A positive number that you want to get the square root of

The SQRT function returns NULL if the number is a negative value.

Here are some examples of how to use SQRT:

SELECT SQRT(25);
Result: 5

SELECT SQRT(26);
Result: 5.0990195135927845

SELECT SQRT(0);
Result: 0

SELECT SQRT(-9);
Result: NULL

Chapter 17: Date and Time Functions

17.1 - ADDDATE

The MySQL ADDDATE function returns a date after which a certain time/date interval has been added.

The syntax for ADDDATE is as follows:

ADDDATE(date, INTERVAL value unit)

OR

ADDDATE(date, days)

date – The date to which the interval should be added.
days – The number of days to add to date (second syntax).
value – The value of the time/date interval that you wish to add. You can specify positive and negative values for this parameter (first syntax).
unit – The unit type of the interval such as DAY, MONTH, MINUTE, HOUR, and so on.

Here are some examples of how to use ADDDATE:

SELECT ADDDATE('2020-05-15', INTERVAL 10 DAY);
Result: '2020-05-25'

SELECT ADDDATE('2020-05-15', 10);
Result: '2020-05-25'

SELECT ADDDATE('2020-02-13', INTERVAL 12 WEEK);
Result: '2020-05-08'

SELECT ADDDATE('2020-02-13', INTERVAL -3 MONTH);

Result: '2019-11-13'

SELECT ADDDATE('2020-02-13', INTERVAL 3 QUARTER);
Result: '2020-11-13'

SELECT ADDDATE('2020-02-13', INTERVAL 5 YEAR);
Result: '2025-02-13'

17.2 - SUBDATE

The MySQL SUBDATE function returns a date after which a certain time/date interval has been subtracted. This function can be viewed as an opposite to ADDDATE.

The syntax for SUBDATE is as follows:

SUBDATE(date, INTERVAL value unit)

OR

SUBDATE(date, days)

date – The date to which the interval should be subtracted.
days – The number of days to subtract from the date (second syntax).
value – The value of the time/date interval that you wish to subtract. You can specify positive and negative values for this parameter (first syntax).
unit – The unit type of the interval such as DAY, MONTH, MINUTE, HOUR, and so on.

Here are some examples of how to use SUBDATE:

SELECT SUBDATE('2020-05-15', INTERVAL 10 DAY);
Result: '2020-05-05'

SELECT SUBDATE('2020-05-15', 10);
Result: '2020-05-05'

SELECT SUBDATE('2020-02-13', INTERVAL 12 WEEK);
Result: '2019-11-21'

SELECT SUBDATE('2020-02-13', INTERVAL 3 MONTH);
Result: '2019-11-13'

SELECT SUBDATE('2020-02-13', INTERVAL 3 QUARTER);
Result: '2019-05-13'

SELECT SUBDATE('2020-02-13', INTERVAL 5 YEAR);
Result: '2015-02-13'

17.3 - ADDTIME

The MySQL ADDTIME function returns a time/datetime value after which a certain time interval has been added.

The syntax for ADDTIME is as follows:

ADDTIME(start_value, time)

start_value – The time or DATETIME value to which the time interval should be added.
time – The value of the time interval that you wish to add. It can be a positive or negative value. As mentioned before, the format for time is 'HH:MM:SS.'
The supported range is '-838:59:59' to '838:59:59.'

Using the ADDTIME function with a negative time value as a parameter is equivalent to using the SUBTIME function.

Here are some examples of how to use ADDTIME:

SELECT ADDTIME('2020-02-13 08:44:21.000001', '2.000001');
Result: '2020-02-13 08:44:23.000002'

SELECT ADDTIME('2020-02-13 08:44:21.000001', '3:2.000001');
Result: '2020-02-13 11:46:21.000002'

SELECT ADDTIME('2020-02-13 08:44:21.000001', '4:3:2.000001');
Result: '2020-02-13 12:47:23.000002'

SELECT ADDTIME('2020-02-13 08:44:21.000001', '5 4:3:2.000001');
Result: '2020-02-18 12:47:23.000002'

SELECT ADDTIME('01:15:23.999998', '0.000001');
Result: '01:15:23.999999'

SELECT ADDTIME('01:15:23.999998', '5.000001');
Result: '01:15:28.999999'

SELECT ADDTIME('01:15:23.000001', '8:12:15.003441');
Result: '09:27:38.003442'

SELECT ADDTIME('01:15:23.000001', '-8:12:15.003441');
Result: '-06:56:52.003440'

17.4 - SUBTIME

The MySQL SUBTIME function returns a time/datetime value after which a certain time interval has been subtracted. This function can be viewed as opposite to ADDTIME.

The syntax for SUBTIME is as follows:

SUBTIME(start_value, time)

start_value – A time or datetime value to which the time interval should be subtracted.
time – The value of the time interval that you wish to subtract. It can be a positive or negative number.

Using the SUBTIME function with a negative time value as a parameter is equivalent to using the ADDTIME function.

Here are some examples of how to use SUBTIME:

SELECT SUBTIME('2020-02-13 08:44:21.000002', '2.000001');
Result: '2020-02-13 08:44:19.000001'

SELECT SUBTIME('2020-02-13 08:44:21.000002', '3:2.000001');
Result: '2020-02-13 05:42:21.000001'

SELECT SUBTIME('2020-02-13 08:44:21.000002', '4:3:2.000001');
Result: '2020-02-13 04:41:19.000001'

SELECT SUBTIME('2020-02-13 08:44:21.000002', '5 4:3:2.000001');
Result: '2020-02-08 04:41:19.000001'

SELECT SUBTIME('01:15:23.999998', '0.000001');
Result: '01:15:23.999997'

SELECT SUBTIME('01:15:23.999998', '5.000001');
Result: '01:15:18.999997'

SELECT SUBTIME('01:15:23.000001', '8:12:15.003441');
Result: '-06:56:52.003440'

SELECT SUBTIME('01:15:23.000001', '-8:12:15.003441');
Result: '09:27:38.003442'

17.5 - CURRENT DATE

The MySQL CURRENT_DATE function returns the current date. This function is useful for many different situations.

The syntax for CURRENT_DATE is as follows:

CURRENT_DATE( )

The CURRENT_DATE function is a synonym for the CURDATE function, both perform the same way.

The CURRENT_DATE function will return the current date as a 'YYYY-MM-DD' format if it is used in a string context.

The CURRENT_DATE function will return the current date as a YYYYMMDD format, if used in a numerical context.

Here are some examples of how to use CURRENT_DATE:

SELECT CURRENT_DATE();
Result: '2020-01-28'

SELECT CURRENT_DATE() + 0;
Result: 20200128

SELECT CURRENT_DATE() + 1;
Result: 20200129

17.6 - CURRENT TIME STAMP

The MySQL CURRENT_TIMESTAMP function returns the current date and time. Use this function if the CURRENT_DATE function does not provide enough detail.

The syntax for CURRENT_TIMESTAMP is as follows:

CURRENT_TIMESTAMP( )

The CURRENT_TIMESTAMP function will return the current date as a 'YYYY-MM-DD HH:MM:SS' format, if used in a string context.

The CURRENT_TIMESTAMP function will return the current date as a YYYYMMDDHHMMSS format, if used in a numeric context in versions of MySQL prior to MySQL 4.1.13.

The CURRENT_TIMESTAMP function will return the current date as a YYYYMMDDHHMMSS.uuuuuu format, if used in a numeric context in versions of MySQL 4.1.13 and newer.

The CURRENT_TIMESTAMP, LOCALTIME, and LOCALTIMESTAMP functions are synonyms for the NOW function.

Here are some examples of how to use CURRENT_TIMESTAMP:

SELECT CURRENT_TIMESTAMP();
Result: '2020-01-28 13:48:41'

SELECT CURRENT_TIMESTAMP() + 0;
Result: 20200128134841.000000

SELECT CURRENT_TIMESTAMP() + 1;
Result: 20200128134842.000000

17.7 - DATE DIFF

The MySQL DATEDIFF function returns the difference in days between two date values.

The syntax for DATEDIFF is as follows:

DATEDIFF(date_1, date_2)

date_1 and *date_2* - The two dates to calculate the difference between.
The calculation is date1 - date2, or date_1 MINUS date_2

Only the date portion of date_1 and date_2 is used in the DATEDIFF calculation. The time portion of date_1 and date_2 is ignored.

Here are some examples of how to use DATEDIFF:

SELECT DATEDIFF('2020-01-28', '2020-01-27');
Result: 1

SELECT DATEDIFF('2020-01-28 11:41:14', '2020-01-27 12:10:08');
Result: 1

SELECT DATEDIFF('2020-01-28 11:41:14', '2020-01-27');
Result: 1

SELECT DATEDIFF('2020-02-15', '2020-02-10');
Result: 5

SELECT DATEDIFF('2020-01-28', '2019-12-31');
Result: 28

SELECT DATEDIFF('2019-12-31', '2020-01-28');
Result: -28

SELECT DATEDIFF(CURDATE(), '2020-02-14');
Result: The difference between the current date, and '2020-02-14'

17.8 - DAY

The MySQL DAY function returns the day portion of a date value.

The syntax for DAY is as follows:

DAY(date_value)

date_value – The date or datetime value from which to extract the day.

The DAY function returns the day of the month (a number from 1 to 31) given a date value.
The DAY function is a synonym for the DAYOFMONTH function.

Here are some examples of how to use DAY:

SELECT DAY('2020-01-28');
Result: 28

SELECT DAY('2020-01-28 15:21:05');
Result: 28

SELECT DAY('2020-10-15');
Result: 15

SELECT DAY(CURDATE())
Result: This would return the current day.

17.9 - WEEK

The MySQL WEEK function returns the week portion of a date value.

The syntax for WEEK is as follows:

WEEK(date_value, [mode])

date_value – A date or datetime value from which to extract the week.
mode – This is an optional parameter. It is used to specify what day the week starts on. It can be one of the following:

Mode	Explanation	Returns
0	First day of the week is Sunday	0-53
1	First day of the week is Monday and the first week has more than 3 days	0-53
2	First day of the week is Sunday	1-53
3	First day of the week is Monday and the first week has more than 3 days	1-53
4	First day of the week is Sunday and the first week has more than 3 days	0-53
5	First day of the week is Monday	0-53
6	First day of the week is Sunday and the first week has more than 3 days	1-53
7	First day of the week is Monday	1-53

The WEEK function will return a value between 0-53 or 1-53 depending on the mode specified.

If you are running MySQL 4.0.14+ and the mode is not specified, the WEEK function will use the value in the default_week_format system variable as the mode.

If you are running a version of MySQL that is older than 4.0.14 and the mode is not specified, the WEEK function will use 0 as the mode.

Here are some examples of how to use WEEK:

SELECT WEEK('2020-01-01');
Result: 0

SELECT WEEK('2020-04-20');
Result: 16

SELECT WEEK('2020-07-16');
Result: 28

SELECT WEEK('2020-10-15');
Result: 41

SELECT WEEK(CURDATE());
Result: This will select the week portion of the current date.

17.10 - MONTH

The MySQL MONTH function returns the month portion of a date value.

The syntax for MONTH is as follows:

MONTH(date_value)

date_value - A date or datetime value from which to extract the month.

The MONTH function returns the month (a number from 1 to 12) given a date value.

Here are some examples of how to use MONTH:

SELECT MONTH('2020-01-28');
Result: 1

SELECT MONTH('2020-01-28 15:21:05');
Result: 1

SELECT MONTH('2020-10-15');
Result: 10

SELECT MONTH(CURDATE());
Result: This will select the month portion of the current date.

17.11 - YEAR

The MySQL YEAR function returns the year portion of a date value.

The syntax for YEAR is as follows:
YEAR(date_value)
date_value - A date or datetime value from which to extract the year.

The YEAR function returns a four-digit year (a number from 1000 to 9999) given a date value.

Here are some examples of how to use YEAR:

SELECT YEAR('2020-01-28');
Result: 2020

SELECT YEAR('2020-01-28 15:21:05');
Result: 2020

SELECT YEAR('2015-10-15');

Result: 2015

SELECT YEAR(CURDATE());
Result: This will select the year portion of the current date.

17.12 - TO_DAYS

The MySQL TO_DAYS function converts a date into numeric days. This is a very useful function. For example, what if we had a user with a one year, or a 365-day long subscription. We can use the TO_DAYS function to see how many days of their subscription remains.

The syntax for TO_DAYS is as follows:

TO_DAYS(date)

date – The date to convert to numeric days.

The TO_DAYS function is to be used only with dates within the Gregorian calendar. The TO_DAYS function will return NULL, if date is '0000-00-00'.

Here are some examples of how to use TO_DAYS:

SELECT TO_DAYS('2014-02-17');
Result: 735646

SELECT TO_DAYS('14-02-17');
Result: 735646

SELECT TO_DAYS('2014-02-18');
Result: 735647

SELECT TO_DAYS('2014-02-19 05:30:00');
Result: 735648

SELECT TO_DAYS('0000-01-01');
Result: 1

```
SELECT TO_DAYS('0000-00-00');
Result: NULL
```

Chapter 18: Final Project

This project integrates all the information you have learned through reading this book. This will test you on your knowledge of MySQL and the various SQL commands and their associated syntax. Let's get started!

Create a database consisting of two connected tables regarding employee information.

```
CREATE TABLE employee_info(
    EmployeeID int PRIMARY KEY,
    FirstName varchar(255),
    LastName varchar(255),
    Title varchar(255)
);
CREATE TABLE salary_info(
    EmployeeID int,
    SalaryYear int,
    SalaryValue float,
    PRIMARY KEY (EmployeeID, SalaryYear),
    FOREIGN KEY (EmployeeID) REFERENCES employee_info (EmployeeID)
);
```

The primary table should be employee_info and should include EmployeeID, FirstName, LastName, and Title.

The second table should be salary_info, containing the EmployeeID, SalaryYear, and SalaryValue (there will be multiple rows per employee if they have multiple years of salary data).

Determine what columns in each table should be Primary and Foreign Keys.

Now that we have created our tables, along with defining our Primary and Foreign Keys, we need to populate our tables with data.

First, insert your rows into the employee_info table. It should look like the following image:

```
1 •    INSERT INTO employee_info(EmployeeID, FirstName, LastName, Title)
2      VALUES (1,'John','Jusge','Senior Manager'),
3             (2,'Aaron','Moore','Manager'),
4             (3,'Sally','Hunter','Administrative Assistance'),
5             (4,'Molly','Potter','CEO'),
6             (5,'Patricia','Culver','Analytics Consultant'),
7             (6,'Leo','Costa','Data Analyst'),
8             (7,'Ryan','Jetson','Human Resources Manager'),
9             (8,'Barbara','Henry','Analytics Consultant'),
10            (9,'Priscilla','Harrison','Manager'),
11            (10,'Alec','Flanders','Data Analyst');
```

Second, insert your rows of data into the salary_info table. It should resemble the SQL command in the image below:

```
1 •    INSERT INTO salary_info(EmployeeID, SalaryYear, SalaryValue)
2      VALUES
3      (1,2019,85700),
4      (2,2018,79000),
5      (3,2019,44000),
6      (4,2018,125600),
7      (5,2019,115000),
8      (6,2019,71000),
9      (7,2019,68200),
10     (8,2019,74700),
11     (9,2018,67000),
12     (10,2019,61500);
```

Now complete the following tasks using the tables you have created!

1. Select all distinct Title names in the database

```
190 ●    SELECT DISTINCT Title FROM employee_info
```

Result Grid | Filter Rows: | Export:

Title
▶ Senior Manager
Manager
Administrative Assistant
CEO
Analytics Consultant
Data Analyst
Human Resources Manager

2. Update one individual to have a mid-year raise and boost their salary in the most recent year by 10%

```
UPDATE salary_info
SET SalaryValue = SalaryValue*1.1
WHERE EmployeeID = 1 and SalaryYear = 2019
```

3. Determine the average salary across all employees in the most recent year in the database. Create a Stored Procedure that will be able to make this calculation based on the year inputted as a parameter.

```
199      DELIMITER //
200 ● ⊖  CREATE PROCEDURE avg_salary_by_year(
201          IN year_of_salary int
202     )
203   ⊖ BEGIN
204          SELECT AVG(SalaryValue) FROM salary_info
205          WHERE SalaryYear = year_of_salary;
206    END //
207      DELIMITER ;
208
209 ●    Call avg_salary_by_year(2019);
210
211
```

| Result Grid | | Filter Rows: | | Export: | | Wrap Cell |

AVG(SalaryValue)
▶ 77038.57142857143

4. Determine the number of employees within each Title who made more than that average salary in the most recent year.

   Hint: a join and a subquery will be necessary!

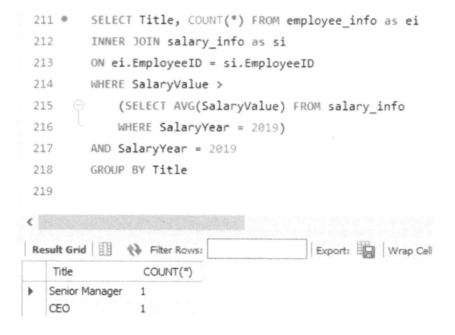

```
211 ●   SELECT Title, COUNT(*) FROM employee_info as ei
212     INNER JOIN salary_info as si
213     ON ei.EmployeeID = si.EmployeeID
214     WHERE SalaryValue >
215   ⊖     (SELECT AVG(SalaryValue) FROM salary_info
216          WHERE SalaryYear = 2019)
217     AND SalaryYear = 2019
218     GROUP BY Title
219
```

| Result Grid | | Filter Rows: | | Export: | | Wrap Cell |

Title	COUNT(*)
▶ Senior Manager	1
CEO	1

18.1 Conclusion

Congratulations! If you have made it this far, you have equipped yourself with an impressive and fundamental knowledge of MySQL. You have acquired a powerful set of skills, which can be applied to many fields and disciplines as well as your own personal projects or business. Understanding the concepts in this book will give you a greater appreciation and understanding of the important role that data plays in our everyday lives. You can now become a part of the new and revolutionary data-driven world!

Made in the USA
Las Vegas, NV
30 March 2022

46561836R00105